The
FEASTS
of the
LORD

The
FEASTS
of the
LORD

Kevin Howard
Marvin Rosenthal

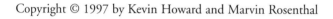

Published in Nashville, Tennessee, by Thomas Nelson, Inc.

Scripture quotations are from THE NEW KING JAMES VERSION of the Bible. Copyright © 1979, 1980, 1982, 1994, Thomas Nelson, Inc., Publishers.

Illustrations by Tom Allen.

ISBN 10: 0-7852-7518-5
ISBN 13: 978-0-7852-7518-3

Printed in the United States of America
07 08 09 10 11 QW 13 12 11 10 9

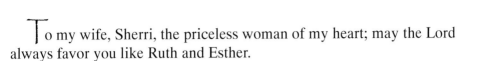

To my wife, Sherri, the priceless woman of my heart; may the Lord always favor you like Ruth and Esther.

To my sons Benjamin and Jared; may the Lord bless you like Ephraim and Manasseh (Gen. 48:20).

To the remnant of Israel; may it be soon, even in our days, that "The remnant will return, the remnant of Jacob, To the Mighty God" (Isa. 10:21).

CONTENTS

ACKNOWLEDGMENTS

We wish to thank the following special friends for allowing the Lord to use their talents and efforts in bringing this book to print:

Staff artist, *Tom Allen,* who with his exciting page layouts and colorful illustrations brought this book to life,

Janice Wills and *Jon Schoenfield* who with their proofing skills identified the myriad of details which needed attention in the text of this book, and

David Rosenthal who with his creative design of the cover attractively brought together the sense of time and *yiddishkeit* (Jewish culture).

May the God of Jacob be pleased with the fruit of our labor: "For the LORD is the great God, And the great King above all gods" (Ps. 95:3).

ISRAEL'S TEMPLE, 1st CENTURY A.D.

The colored location dots are referenced throughout the book.

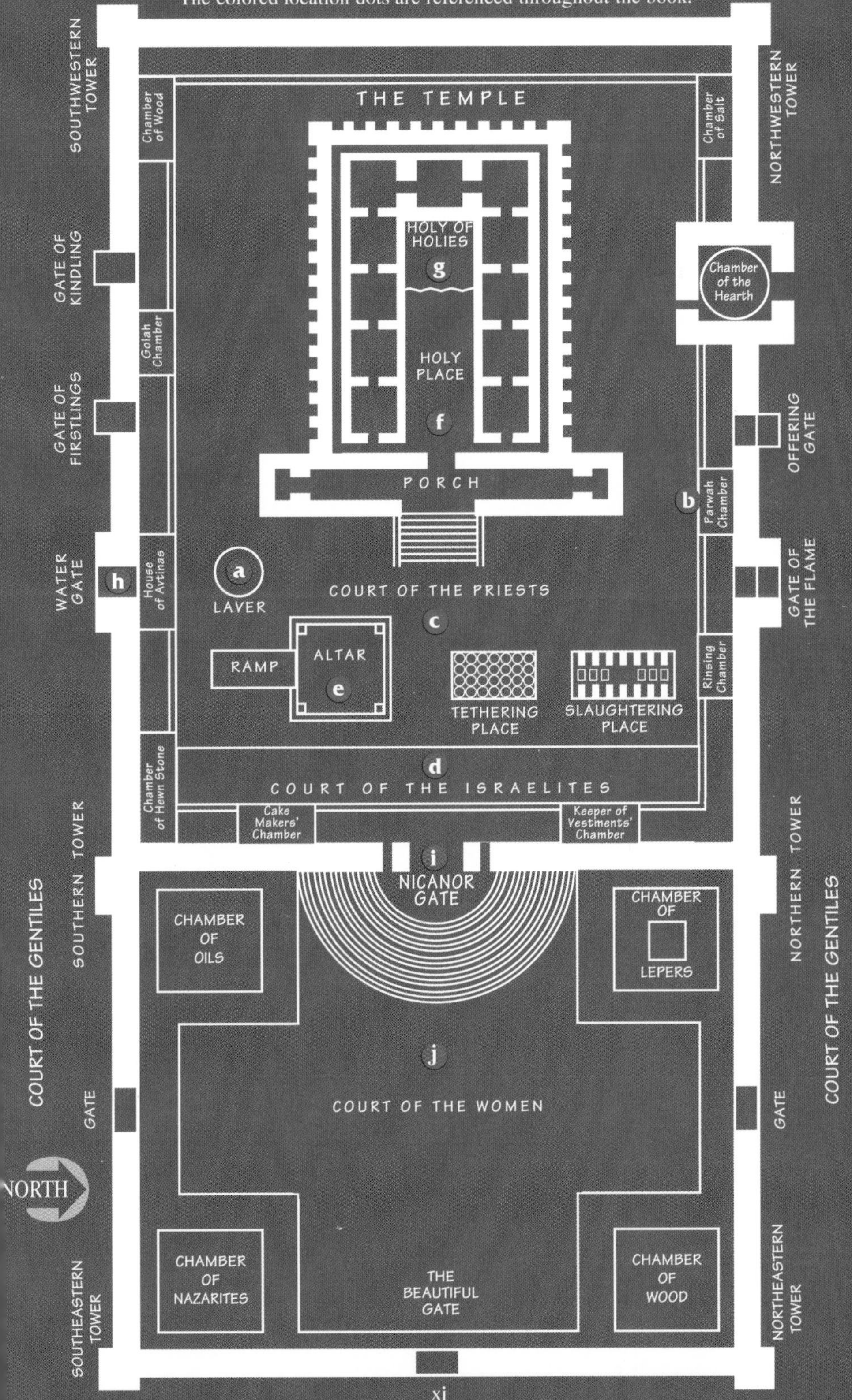

SOUTHWESTERN TOWER

NORTHWESTERN TOWER

Chamber of Wood

Chamber of Salt

THE TEMPLE

GATE OF KINDLING

HOLY OF HOLIES

g

Golah Chamber

Chamber of the Hearth

GATE OF FIRSTLINGS

HOLY PLACE

f

OFFERING GATE

House of Avtinas

PORCH

Parwah Chamber

GATE OF THE FLAME

WATER GATE

h

a

LAVER

b

COURT OF THE PRIESTS

c

Rinsing Chamber

Chamber of Hewn Stone

RAMP

ALTAR

e

TETHERING PLACE

SLAUGHTERING PLACE

d

COURT OF THE ISRAELITES

SOUTHERN TOWER

Cake Makers' Chamber

Keeper of Vestments' Chamber

NORTHERN TOWER

i

NICANOR GATE

COURT OF THE GENTILES

CHAMBER OF OILS

CHAMBER OF LEPERS

COURT OF THE GENTILES

GATE

j

GATE

COURT OF THE WOMEN

NORTH

SOUTHEASTERN TOWER

CHAMBER OF NAZARITES

THE BEAUTIFUL GATE

CHAMBER OF WOOD

NORTHEASTERN TOWER

"'These are the feasts of the Lord, holy convocations, which you shall proclaim at their appointed times'" (Lev. 23:4).

Overview of the Spring Feasts

Marvin J. Rosenthal

Men the world over observe holidays. There is not a nation anywhere, even among the most primitive of peoples, that does not have its unique days of special celebration. Holidays are often in memory of significant political events; sometimes they commemorate the birth dates of national heroes; and frequently, holidays are simply designed to observe religious beliefs and superstitions. Worldwide, thousands of holidays are observed annually.

In marked contrast, the eternal God instituted only seven holidays. And while it is not inappropriate for men to establish days of special celebration, their significance cannot be compared with the importance of the seven holidays instituted by God. These seven holidays are discussed throughout the Bible, in both the Old and New Testaments. However, only in one place, the twenty-third chapter of Leviticus, are all seven holidays listed in chronological sequence.

These seven holidays are called "the feasts of the Lord." That expression indicates that these holidays are God's holidays — they belong to Him — in contrast to man's holidays. They are, quite literally, "the feasts of the LORD" (Lev. 23:4). And only on His terms and at His invitation can men participate in them and enter into their benefits.

The Hebrew word translated "feasts" means *appointed times*. The idea is that the sequence and timing of each of these feasts have been carefully orchestrated by God himself. Each is part of a comprehensive whole. Collectively, they tell a story. These feasts are also called "holy convocations"; that is, they are intended to be times of meeting between God and man for "holy purposes." Since these seven feasts of the Lord are "appointed times" for "holy purposes," they carry with them great sacredness and solemnity.

A number of important points need to be emphasized concerning these feasts.

FIRST, these seven feasts of the Lord were given to the Hebrew nation. The Jewish people are God's covenant people.

■ SECOND, these seven feasts relate to Israel's spring and fall agricultural seasons. When the feasts were instituted, Israel was largely an agricultural nation. That agricultural characteristic of the feasts remains to this day.

■ THIRD, the timing of these seven feasts is based on the Jewish lunar (moon) calendar of approximately 354-day years. Periodically (seven times every nineteen years), the modern Jewish calendar literally has a thirteenth month to make up for its shorter year. If such were not the case, winter months on the Jewish calendar would soon occur in the summer, and summer months in the winter. It is for this reason that these holidays do not fall on the same day on the Gregorian calendar (the calendar commonly used today) each year.

■ FOURTH and fundamentally, these seven feasts typify the sequence, timing, and significance of the major events of the Lord's redemptive career. They commence at Calvary where Jesus voluntarily gave Himself for the sins of the world (Passover), and climax at the establishment of the messianic Kingdom at the Messiah's second coming (Tabernacles). No box has to be manufactured, no text twisted, and no truth manipulated to make these appointed feasts conform to specific events in the Messiah's life.

■ FIFTH, because the spiritual realities to which the feasts clearly point are fulfilled in Messiah, all men everywhere have been placed in an opportune position. All of humanity has been extended an invitation to "meet" with God and receive the blessings toward which these seven feasts unerringly point. To turn down this unprecedented and gracious invitation is the height of folly.

■ SIXTH, the participation of Gentiles in the blessing associated with the feasts God appointed for Israel should come as no surprise. It is consistent with God's unconditional covenant to the patriarch Abraham, the central provision of which is, "In your seed all the nations of the earth shall be blessed" (Gen. 22:18). The Messiah himself taught, "Salvation is of the Jews" (Jn. 4:22). Israel and the Church are distinct entities with distinct promises. However, every blessing which the true Church now enjoys and every hope which she anticipates come out of the Abrahamic, Davidic, and New Covenants which God made with Israel. There is a contiguous relationship between Israel and the Church. Therefore, it should not be thought that Gentiles cannot enter into the blessings which were accomplished through the Messiah and to which the feasts point.

There is hardly a theme to which a man can give his attention that is loftier or more important than the seven feasts of the Lord. Permit it to be said once more, for its importance warrants it: These seven feasts depict the entire redemptive career of the Messiah.

"Seven" is the biblical number for perfection and completion. After creating the world, God rested on the seventh day. He did not rest as a consequence of growing tired — omnipotence does not grow tired, and God is omnipotent. Rather, God rested in the sense of *completion* and *satisfaction*. What God created was *good* and *satisfying* — nothing else was needed. Therefore, He rested on the seventh day.

• On the seventh day of the week, the children of Israel were to observe a Sabbath rest, patterned after God's creation rest. They were to rest from all their labors (Ex. 16:23, 30).

• The seventh month of the year is, according to the Scriptures, especially holy. In that month, all three fall feasts are observed (Lev. 23:24, 27, 34).

• The nation of Israel was commanded to refrain from farming the ground every seventh year — to allow the soil to rest (Lev. 25:4).

• Seven sevens of years were counted (forty-nine years), and then the next year (the fiftieth) was to be the Jubilee year in which all debts were forgiven and all slaves set free (Lev. 25:8-12).

• Seventy sevens of years were "determined" upon the Jewish people during which time God would bring to perfection and completion His redemptive purposes (Dan. 9:24-27).

• The Book of Revelation records the consummation of this age. It uses the number *seven* more than fifty times. Significantly, the book revolves around seven seals, seven trumpets, and seven bowls (Rev. 5:1, 5; 6; 8-9; 11:15-19; 15-16).

The seven feasts of the Lord, then, are His "appointed times" during which He will meet with men for holy purposes. When completed, the seven holidays will bring this age to a triumphant end and usher in the "Golden Age" to follow. During that age, every man will sit under his own fig tree (Mic. 4:4). That concept is not intended to suggest boredom or a lack of creativity and activity, but completion and satisfaction. In that day, every good thing that the heart could desire will be possessed.

Four of the seven holidays occur in the spring of the year. The fulfillment of those feasts, if a colloquialism may be used to emphasize the truth, are "a done deal." That is to say, the events which the four spring feasts of the Lord typify in the Hebrew Scriptures have been fulfilled in the Messiah. In that sense, one can look back at and examine them. They are history. They occurred almost two thousand years ago. Their spiritual benefits, however, continue forward to the present hour.

The final three holidays occur in the fall of the year within a brief period in the Hebrew month of Tishri (September/October). As the first four holidays depict events associated with Messiah's first coming, these final three holidays depict specific events associated with His second coming. Although these events are still future in terms of literal fulfillment, biblical faith may lay hold of and live in the light of their future blessings today. These final feasts form the basis for what the Bible calls the "blessed hope" (Ti. 2:13).

The four spring feasts, with which this chapter is concerned, are summed up in the short span of nineteen verses of Scripture (Lev. 23:4-22).

THE FEAST OF PASSOVER

The first "feast of the LORD" is *Passover* (Lev. 23:5). It is the foundational feast. The six feasts that follow are built upon it.

Passover occurs in the spring of the year, on the fourteenth day of the Hebrew month, Nisan (March/April). In the same way that many colleges have academic years and businesses have fiscal years, the month in which Passover occurs commences the religious year for Israel.

While the Jewish people have celebrated the Passover annually since the time of Moses, in reality, there was only one Passover. It occurred almost 3,500 years ago in Egypt. It was there, at that time, that a lamb was sacrificed and the blood was applied to each doorpost and lintel. When this was done in faith and in obedience to God's command, that home was "passed over," and the life of the firstborn was spared. All subsequent observances over the centuries have been memorials of that one and only first Passover.

In precisely the same way, there was only one occasion when the Messiah's flesh was pierced and His blood spilled on the cross of Calvary for the sin of the world. The Lord's Supper is an ongoing memorial of that one momentous occasion.

The events leading up to the Passover are among the most dramatic in all of Scripture.

The children of Israel were enslaved in Egypt. Pharaoh was a harsh taskmaster. The lot of the Hebrews seemed hopeless. It was at that hour of history that God spoke to Moses from within a burning bush. It was a desert area — the bush was dry and sapless. Everything normal and natural argued for the speedy consumption of that thornbush. But such was not the case. The bush burned and was not consumed (Ex. 3:2). Not without reason, therefore, Moses turned aside to see this unusual sight. And from the midst of that burning bush, God would speak to His servant.

That burning bush typified Israel. Through the centuries, she would experience the hot flames of satanic fury, often manifested in the form of vehement anti-Semitism — she would burn, but she would not be consumed. And as God spoke to Moses from the midst of a burning bush, He has spoken to the world amidst the fiery trials of Israel. She alone was the depository of God's Word to man. When holy men of God spoke as they were borne along by the Holy Spirit, they were Jewish men.

God would tell Moses that He had seen the affliction of His people down in Egypt, that He had heard their cry for help, that He knew their sorrows. And now, He was coming down to deliver them out of Egyptian bondage and to bring them into the Promised Land (Ex. 3:7-8).

At that moment, the Hebrews were a motley group of unorganized and uneducated slaves. They knew nothing of nationhood yet — that would happen at Mount Sinai. They carried about, under their nails and in their hair, the mud of the slime pits of Egypt. There was nothing innately desirable about this group of unkempt slaves who had, through the years, all but forgotten their God. Lesser gods, gods created by men's minds and fashioned by their hands from wood and stone, would have passed them by. After all, the sons of Jacob had not been faithful to their God.

It could have been argued that He owed them nothing, that He was no man's debtor. But not the true and living God. He was the God of Abraham, Isaac, and Jacob. And to them He had solemnly promised that their seed would be as the sand of the seashore and the stars of the heaven — without number. God is a covenant-keeping God. What His mouth speaks, His right arm of power performs. Therefore, the Hebrews, however unattractive and undesirable they may have appeared at that moment, were still "His people." He was aware of their affliction, and by His reckoning, it was time for them to "pack their bags and head for home" after more than four hundred years in Egypt.

Cecil B. deMille, in his classic epic, *The Ten Commandments*, while using the best cinematography and special effects of his day, did not overstate the reality of the exodus from Egypt. Nor could men today, with all of their technology, in a remake of *The Ten Commandments*, overstate the miraculous nature of the exodus.

The eternal God was at work. He hardened Pharaoh's heart so that he would not let the children of Israel go. And then, plague after plague was unleashed with deadly accuracy against the idolatrous land of Egypt. Each of the plagues was directed against an Egyptian deity, until, at last, the firstborn of each home in Egypt would perish where a lamb was not slain and the blood was not applied. The plague reached even to the palace of Pharaoh himself. Since the pharaoh of Egypt was worshiped as a god, a god's son would die.

Finally, in desperation, Pharaoh consented to let the children of Israel go. Under Moses, servant of the Lord, it is estimated that more than a million slaves, with all of their possessions, marched past the Sphinx of Egypt into the desert. What a scene that must have been to behold! What insanity by human standards! A million emancipated slaves marching off into the desert. Unlike most ancient cities, there was no great wall surrounding the nation of Egypt. None was necessary. The inhospitable desert provided the best protection. And here were the Hebrews, walking right into it — men, women, children, and livestock. Water, food, shelter, clothing — from where would these most basic necessities come? These Hebrews, as they were known at that time, knew little about where they were going or how they would get there. However, Moses knew the One who was leading them. They would cross the Red Sea, they would wander in the wilderness for forty years, and ultimately, under Joshua, they would enter the promised land.

Of the many words that could be used to describe what took place in Egypt 3,500 years ago, none fits better or is more comprehensive than the one word, *redemption*. The events were real, the miracles genuine — all wrought by the God of the Hebrews, who was greater than all the gods of Egypt.

A motley crew of slaves was *redeemed* so that they could worship and serve the true and living God. But such a redemption was not without cost. Blood had to be shed to secure their redemption.

All of those lambs sacrificed down in Egypt (one per household) pointed to the one true Lamb of God who takes away the sin of the world (Jn. 1:29). Writing to the Corinthians, the apostle Paul noted for all of time that "Christ, our Passover, was sacrificed for us" (1 Cor. 5:7). "Low in the grave He lay!"

 # THE FEAST OF UNLEAVENED BREAD

God appointed another feast which was to begin the very next day after Passover, on the fifteenth of the Hebrew month, Nisan. It is called the "Feast of Unleavened Bread." It was to last for seven days. On the first night, and again on the seventh, there was to be a time of meeting (convocation) between God and man. So intimately related are these first two holidays, Passover and Unleavened Bread, that with the passing of time they came to be observed as one holiday by the Jewish people.

I can remember vividly, how, when I was young, my orthodox Jewish grandmother, in preparation for the Feast of Unleavened Bread, would meticulously go throughout the house sprinkling bread crumbs (leaven/yeast) at difficult-to-get-at places in literally every room in the house. Then, armed with only a broom and a dustpan, she would march through the house sweeping the leaven (which she herself had recently scattered throughout the house) into the kitchen. She would then sweep the crumbs into the dust pan, take it out of the house, and burn it. Even today, in observant Jewish homes throughout the world, this ancient custom is still observed. It is, as expressed in the words of *Fiddler on the Roof*, "tradition."

In the Bible, leaven symbolizes error or evil. It is the agent that causes fermentation. The Lord said to His disciples, "Beware of the leaven [erroneous doctrine] of the Pharisees" (Mt. 16:6, 11; Mk. 8:15). And the apostle Paul warned the Corinthian church, in a context of unjudged sin in their midst, that "a little leaven [yeast] leavens [ferments] the whole lump" (1 Cor. 5:6). Left undealt with, sin will permeate and infect everything.

The Messiah was crucified on Passover. For His Roman executioners, the Jewish holy day was no barrier to carrying out their dastardly task (Mt. 26:5). He was then taken from the cross and, in keeping with Jewish custom, buried as soon as possible. His body was placed in a borrowed tomb — the tomb of Joseph of Arimathaea. But, unlike all other corpses, His body would not decay in the grave. There would be no decomposition of His flesh. His body would be exempted from the divine pronouncement that from the dust of the ground man came and to the dust of the ground he shall return (Gen. 3:19). This truth should not catch us off guard. Did not the Messiah allow us to listen in on a conversation He had with His Father: "You will not leave my soul in Hades [sheol], Nor will You allow Your Holy One to see corruption [to decompose in the grave]" (Acts 2:27; cf. Ps. 16:10)?

If Passover speaks of the Lord's death on Calvary — and it does so, loudly and clearly — the Feast of Unleavened Bread proclaims that His physical body would not experience the ravages of death while in the grave.

THE FEAST OF FIRSTFRUITS

The third feast occurs on the second day of the seven-day Feast of Unleavened Bread. It is called the "Feast of Firstfruits." Passover occurs on the fourteenth of Nisan; the first day of the "Feast of Unleavened Bread" occurs on the fifteenth; and "Firstfruits," according to Jewish reckoning, occurs on the sixteenth day of the Hebrew month, Nisan.

The barley harvest — the first crop planted in the winter — is now, in the spring, beginning to ripen.

The first sheaf (firstfruits) of the harvest is cut and, in a carefully pre-scribed and meticulous ceremony, presented to the Lord. The Lord's acceptance of the firstfruits is an "earnest," or pledge, on His part of a full harvest. As to the significance of the Feast of Firstfruits, as with the other feasts, there is no room for doubt or speculation.

In writing to the church at Corinth, the apostle Paul found it necessary to correct a major doctrinal error which was creeping into the assembly of believers. Some were being infected by the deadly first-century virus known as "gnosticism." Among other things, this philosophy held that the material universe was inherently evil. Consequently, if men rose physically from the grave, according to gnosticism, the result would be an evil body. Because of this teaching, some within the Church were beginning to deny the concept of physical resurrection. They believed in the immortality of the soul, but not in the resurrection of the body. The apostle Paul rushed to "nip the problem in the bud." He wrote to the Corinthian believers: "Now if Christ is preached that he has been raised from the dead, how do some among you say that there is no resurrection of the dead?" (1 Cor. 15:12). To reject the concept of physical resurrec-tion was to reject the physical resurrection of Christ. Logically, you can't have the latter without the former.

To DENY PHYSICAL RESURRECTION was to call the apostle Paul a liar, for he had taught them that Messiah rose bodily from the grave. To the Corinthians, Paul wrote: "For I delivered to you first of all that which I also received: that Christ died for our sins according to the Scriptures, and that He was buried, and that He rose again the third day according to the Scriptures" (1 Cor. 15:3-4).

To DENY THE PHYSICAL RESURRECTION OF MESSIAH was to repudiate their faith. Paul argued, "And if Christ is not risen, then our preaching is empty, and your faith is also empty" (1 Cor. 15:14).

To DENY THE PHYSICAL RESURRECTION OF MESSIAH was to consign loved ones who had died in Christ to eternal condemnation. Paul noted, "Then also those who have fallen asleep in Christ have perished" (1 Cor. 15:18).

To DENY THE PHYSICAL RESURRECTION OF MESSIAH was to consign men to misery. Paul warned, "If in this life only we have hope in Christ [and such would be the case if there were no bodily resurrection], we are of all men the most pitiable" (1 Cor. 15:19).

Using irresistible logic, Paul brought those denying bodily resurrection down to the depths of despair based on their own reasoning.

The Corinthians' thesis was this: There is no bodily resurrection.

Paul's valid conclusion was: Then Messiah is not raised.

The tragic consequence of their thesis, if correct, would be this inescapable conclusion: Paul was a liar, their faith was in vain, their loved ones who had died in the Lord had perished, and they were of all men most miserable. Happily, their thesis was not correct.

Using one word (two words in the English), Paul leapt from the depths of despair (where a denial of physical resurrection unerringly led them) to the heights of certain hope and exaltation. Those two English words are "but now." Paul wrote, "**But now** Christ is risen from the dead" (1 Cor. 15:20). The apostle Paul loved to use the expression, "but now." He used it no less than eighteen times in the New Testament (1 Cor. 12:18, 20; 15:20; 2 Cor. 8:22; 12:6; Gal. 4:9; Eph. 2:13; 5:8; Phil. 2:12; Col. 1:26; 3:8; 2 Tim. 1:10; Phile. 11; Heb. 2:8; 8:6; 9:26; 11:16; 12:26). When he did so, he often used it as an equivalent to the military terms, "About face!" or "To the rear, march!" He was saying, "Turn around one hundred eighty degrees."

For instance, to the church at Ephesus, Paul wrote: "That at that time you were without Christ, being aliens from the commonwealth of Israel and strangers from the covenants of promise, having no hope and without God in the world. **But now** in Christ Jesus you who once were far off have been brought near by the blood of Christ" (Eph. 2:12-13). And again: "For you were once darkness, **but now** you are light in the Lord. Walk as children of light" (Eph. 5:8). And to the Philippians, he wrote: "Therefore, my beloved, as you have always obeyed, not as in my presence only, **but now** much more in my absence, work out your own salvation with fear and trembling" (Phil. 2:12).

Some were saying that there is no physical resurrection of the dead. Logically, therefore, Messiah was not resurrected. The end result of such thinking is hopelessness and despair. Paul's triumphant response was: **"But now** Christ is risen from the dead, and has become the firstfruits of those who have fallen asleep" (1 Cor. 15:20). Paul had in mind the first sheaf (firstfruits) of the barley harvest (Lev. 23:10). When God accepted the firstfruits, they became the *earnest* or *guarantee* that the rest of the crop would be harvested. Christ himself is the "firstfruits" (1 Cor. 15:23). In both the Old and New Testaments, there were people who were raised from the dead (1 Ki. 17:17-23; 2 Ki. 4:18-37; Lk. 8:54-55; Jn. 11:43-44). In time, however, they died again. Jesus was the first to be resurrected from the grave, never to die again. He alone is the "firstfruits."

The feast of Passover spoke of Messiah's death as a sacrificial and substitutionary lamb.

The Feast of Unleavened Bread indicated that His body would not decay in the grave.

The Feast of Firstfruits proclaims that death could not hold her Foe. "Up from the grave He arose, with a mighty triumph o'er His foes."

THE FEAST OF WEEKS

The fourth feast is known as *Shavuot* (Hebrew), "Weeks." It is called the Feast of Weeks because God specifically told the sons of Jacob that they were to count seven weeks from Firstfruits (Lev. 23:15; Dt. 16:9), and then on the "day after" this fourth feast was to be observed (Lev. 23:16). Seven weeks are forty-nine days. Add one day ("the day after"), and it brings the total to fifty days. This fourth feast was to occur precisely fifty days after Firstfruits (Messiah's resurrection). This feast is also called "Pentecost" (Acts 2:1) — meaning "fiftieth."

On this occasion, the children of Israel were not simply to bring the first-fruits of the wheat harvest to the Temple (as they brought the firstfruits of the barley at the Feast of Firstfruits), but two loaves of bread. These two loaves of bread were to be baked with fine flour and leaven.

Fifty days, two loaves, leaven — what did it all mean? In short, it all pointed to the coming of the Holy Spirit and the birthday of the Church. The Son of God arose from the grave on Firstfruits. He then spent forty days with His disciples in postresurrection ministry (Acts 1:3). He informed them that it was necessary that He ascend to His Father (there to apply the benefits of His once-and-for-all sacrifice), but that He would not abandon them. He would send them His Holy Spirit who would come alongside to help in His absence (Jn. 14:16-17).

They were commanded to *tarry* at Jerusalem until He came (Acts 1:4). They waited as they were commanded. Their wait was not long — only ten days. And then it happened: the Spirit of God descended on those first-century believers.

For the Feast of Weeks, two loaves were brought to the Temple. They represented Jew and Gentile, now one in the Messiah with the coming of the Holy Spirit. Writing to the Ephesian believers, Paul said: "For He Himself is our peace, who has made both [Jew and Gentile] one, and has broken down the middle wall of separation . . . to create in Himself one new man from the two [Jew and Gentile], thus making peace" (Eph. 2:14-15).

There was to be leaven in those two loaves, for the believers have not yet been glorified. During this age, there is still sin within the Church. Someone has rightly said of believers, "If you find a perfect church, don't join it because you will spoil it." Positionally in the Savior, the Church is perfected. Practically or experientially, she still has a long way to go.

Messiah, the head, is unleavened. The Church, the body, still has leaven within her. Therefore, leaven was to be included in those two loaves.

The Fulfillment of the Spring Feasts

Passover speaks of *redemption*. Messiah, the Passover Lamb, has been slain for us.

Unleavened Bread speaks of *sanctification*. He was set apart. His body would not decay in the grave.

Firstfruits speaks of *resurrection*. Death could not hold her Foe. On the third day, Jesus rose triumphantly from the grave.

The Feast of Weeks speaks of *origination*. The coming of the Holy Spirit inaugurated the New Covenant and Church Age which the Messiah instituted in the Upper Room (Mt. 26:28-29). The middle wall of separation between Jews and Gentiles has been broken down. From the two, the Lord is calling out the Church, which is His body.

Each major event of the Messiah's first coming occurred on the precise date of the appropriate Jewish holiday. Each of the three major events to be associated with His second coming will, likewise, fall on the appropriate Jewish holiday. Those three feasts — Trumpets, the Day of Atonement, and Tabernacles — unerringly point to the Rapture of the Church and judgment of the wicked, the salvation of Israel, and the establishment of the messianic Kingdom.

רֹאשׁ הַשָּׁנָה

יוֹם כִּפּוּר

סֻכּוֹת

"Speak to the children of Israel, saying:
'In the seventh month . . . '" (Lev. 23:24).

Overview of the Fall Feasts

Marvin J. Rosenthal

The redemptive work of Messiah's first coming, which the four spring feasts depict, is history. Men can look back at these events, and they can be examined as historical facts. The three fall feasts have not yet been fulfilled. They predict, with absolute certainty, events that will yet unfold. As the four spring holidays were fulfilled literally and right on schedule in connection with Messiah's first coming, the three fall holidays will likewise be fulfilled literally and right on schedule in connection with His second coming.

THE FEAST OF TRUMPETS

The Feast of Trumpets is the first of the fall feasts. It is called Rosh Hashanah by the Jewish people. *Rosh Hashanah* literally means "Head of the Year" and is observed as the start of the *civil* year (in contrast to the *religious* year which starts just prior to Passover) on the Jewish calendar. However, this designation was never given to the Feast of Trumpets in the Bible. The idea of associating the Feast of Trumpets with the Jewish New Year began in the second century A.D. (shortly after the destruction of the Temple) and more than 1,500 years after its inception in the time of Moses. The Feast of Trumpets is so important in Jewish thinking that it stands alongside *Yom Kippur* ("the Day of Atonement") to comprise what Judaism calls "the high holy days."

The interval of time between the last of the spring feasts (Pentecost) and the first of the fall feasts (Trumpets) corresponds to this present age. Put another way, we are presently living between Israel's fourth and fifth feasts. The outpouring of the Holy Spirit at Pentecost commenced the Church Age; and Trumpets, which will signal Messiah's second coming to rapture the Church and judge the wicked, will end the Church Age.

In Israel's religious ritual, she utilized two different kinds of trumpets. One was long and flared and made of silver (Num. 10:2). The other was a ram's horn and is called, in Hebrew, the *shofar*. It is this second instrument which is utilized in the elaborate service connected with the Feast of Trumpets.

The blowing of the trumpet in ancient Israel had two primary functions. The first was to call a solemn assembly; that is, when the children of Israel were to be summoned to God's presence, the trumpet was blown (Ex. 19:13, 17, 19; Num. 10:2). And second, when Israel, under divine direction, was to go to war, the trumpet was to be blown (Num. 10:9; Jud. 7; Jer. 4:19-21). Joshua blew the shofar in the conquest of Jericho (Josh. 6:20). Gideon blew the trumpet in the battle with the Midianites (Jud. 7:18). Nehemiah commanded that the trumpet be blown in the event of attack when rebuilding the walls of Jerusalem (Neh. 4:18).

The prophets of Israel repeatedly spoke of a future day when God would directly intervene in the affairs of men. They called that day "the Day of the Lord" (Isa. 13:6-13; Ezek. 13:3-8; 30:2-3; Joel 1:15; 3:14-16; Amos 5:18-20; Zeph. 1:14-2:3; Zech. 14:1-4; Mal. 4:5-6). Two major themes are associated with the Day of the Lord. The first is the deliverance of the righteous. The second is the judgment of the wicked. In connection with His coming, the Messiah will call His own to Himself and then go to war against His enemies. It is the blowing of a trumpet which will signal those two events. In the classic Rapture text of 1 Thessalonians 4, the Lord will descend with the sound of the trumpet to call His own to His presence; and then, as seen in chapter 5, the Day of the Lord will commence, during which time His wrath will be poured out against the wicked.

In most basic terms, the Feast of Trumpets — the first of the three fall feasts — depicts the coming of the Messiah to rapture the Church and judge the wicked.

Some balk and argue that these feasts were given to Israel, not the Church, therefore, the Feast of Trumpets cannot depict the Rapture. In response, we make the following observations, to which many more could be added:

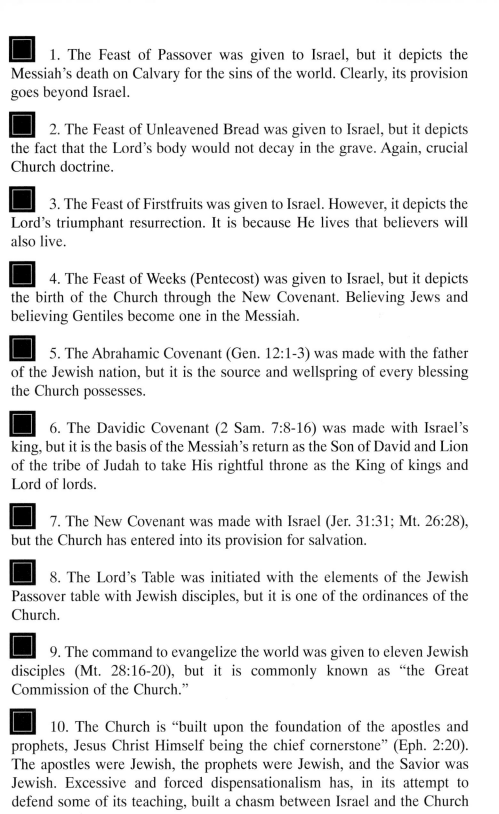

■ 1. The Feast of Passover was given to Israel, but it depicts the Messiah's death on Calvary for the sins of the world. Clearly, its provision goes beyond Israel.

■ 2. The Feast of Unleavened Bread was given to Israel, but it depicts the fact that the Lord's body would not decay in the grave. Again, crucial Church doctrine.

■ 3. The Feast of Firstfruits was given to Israel. However, it depicts the Lord's triumphant resurrection. It is because He lives that believers will also live.

■ 4. The Feast of Weeks (Pentecost) was given to Israel, but it depicts the birth of the Church through the New Covenant. Believing Jews and believing Gentiles become one in the Messiah.

■ 5. The Abrahamic Covenant (Gen. 12:1-3) was made with the father of the Jewish nation, but it is the source and wellspring of every blessing the Church possesses.

■ 6. The Davidic Covenant (2 Sam. 7:8-16) was made with Israel's king, but it is the basis of the Messiah's return as the Son of David and Lion of the tribe of Judah to take His rightful throne as the King of kings and Lord of lords.

■ 7. The New Covenant was made with Israel (Jer. 31:31; Mt. 26:28), but the Church has entered into its provision for salvation.

■ 8. The Lord's Table was initiated with the elements of the Jewish Passover table with Jewish disciples, but it is one of the ordinances of the Church.

■ 9. The command to evangelize the world was given to eleven Jewish disciples (Mt. 28:16-20), but it is commonly known as "the Great Commission of the Church."

■ 10. The Church is "built upon the foundation of the apostles and prophets, Jesus Christ Himself being the chief cornerstone" (Eph. 2:20). The apostles were Jewish, the prophets were Jewish, and the Savior was Jewish. Excessive and forced dispensationalism has, in its attempt to defend some of its teaching, built a chasm between Israel and the Church which the Bible never sanctions.

Israel and the Church are distinct entities. The Church is not Israel, and Israel is not the Church. There are promises made to both. It is equally clear, however, that there is a contiguous relationship between Israel and the Church. Every blessing which the Church enjoys comes out of covenants and provisions which God made with Israel. Therefore, it should not seem strange or unusual that the Feast of Trumpets which the Lord gave to Israel should depict the Rapture of the Church immediately prior to the outpouring of God's wrath during the Day of the Lord.

Perhaps one further thought is appropriate at this point. The Feast of Trumpets occurs on the first day of the Hebrew month of Tishri. It occurs at the New Moon when only the slightest crescent is visible. However, clouds could obscure the moon, and witnesses were required in ancient days. Watchfulness was a critical ingredient of this feast. The rabbis later added a second day to this feast to make sure they did not miss it. This need for watchfulness and preparedness in connection with the Feast of Trumpets is echoed and reechoed throughout the New Testament in connection with Messiah's coming.

Watch, therefore, for you do not know what hour your Lord is coming (Mt. 24:42).

Therefore let us not sleep, as others do, but let us watch and be sober (1 Th. 5:6).

Looking for the blessed hope and glorious appearing of our great God and Savior Jesus Christ (Ti. 2:13).

So Christ was offered once to bear the sins of many. To those who eagerly wait for Him He will appear a second time, apart from sin, for salvation (Heb. 9:28).

Looking for and hastening the coming of the day of God, because of which the heavens will be dissolved, being on fire, and the elements will melt with fervent heat? Nevertheless we, according to His promise, look for new heavens and a new earth in which righteousness dwells. Therefore, beloved, looking forward to these things, be diligent to be found by Him in peace, without spot and blameless (2 Pet. 3:12-14).

Whereas Trumpets occurred on the first day of the Hebrew month of Tishri at the New Moon, the Day of Atonement occurred nine days later on the tenth of the month. The ten days from Trumpets through the Day of Atonement are known as "the days of awe."

According to Jewish tradition, three books are opened in heaven on the Feast of Trumpets. One is the Book of Life for the righteous. The second is the Book of Life for the unrighteous. The third is the Book of Life for those in-between. If a man is deemed righteous, his name is written in the Book of Life for the righteous at the Feast of Trumpets. If a man is unrighteous, his name is written in the Book of Life for the unrighteous, and he will not survive the year. If a man is deemed in-between, judgment is delayed from the Feast of Trumpets to the Day of Atonement. It is during that period of time that he is given opportunity to repent before the book is closed and his destiny sealed.

While I will not be dogmatic on this issue, I strongly believe that at the Feast of Trumpets, the Church will be raptured and the Lord's wrath will commence on the earth. The outpouring of the Lord's wrath will occupy a relatively brief period of time. At His physical return to the earth, many Jews who survived the Lord's purging of the earth will be saved. The prophet Zechariah wrote of that event this way: "It shall be in that day that I will seek to destroy all the nations that come against Jerusalem. And I will pour on the house of David and on the inhabitants of Jerusalem the Spirit of grace and supplication; then they will look on Me whom they pierced. Yes, they will mourn for Him as one mourns for his only son, and grieve for Him as one grieves for a firstborn" (Zech. 12:9-10). And Paul, in the context of a believing remnant from among the nation of Israel at the end of the age, wrote: "For I do not desire, brethren, that you should be ignorant of this mystery, lest you should be wise in your own opinion, that blindness in part has happened to Israel until the fullness of the Gentiles has come in. And so all Israel will be saved, as it is written: 'The Deliverer will come out of Zion, And He will turn away ungodliness from Jacob'" (Rom. 11:25-26).

But it will not only be Israel's Day of Atonement. From among the nations of the world, many individuals will not take the mark of the Antichrist. And when the Lord Jesus returns to the earth, many will repent of their sins before the Book of Life is forever closed. The Lord had these Gentiles in mind in His Olivet Discourse. He taught:

> When the Son of Man comes in His glory, and all the holy angels with Him, then He will sit on the throne of His glory. All the nations will be gathered before Him, and He will separate them one from another, as a shepherd divides his sheep from the goats. And He will set the sheep on His right hand, but the goats on the left. Then the King will say to those on His right hand, "Come, you blessed of My Father, inherit the kingdom prepared for you from the foundation of the world" (Mt. 25:31-34).

It is this multitude from among the nations, along with those from among the sons of Jacob, who will enter the messianic Kingdom still in mortal bodies (as distinct from the raptured and glorified Church who will inhabit New Jerusalem).

THE FEAST OF TABERNACLES

On the fifteenth of Tishri, the seven-day Feast of Tabernacles commences. It is the seventh and final feast. It usually occurs in October. Observant Jews erect little "huts" or "booths" from bulrushes as a reminder of the temporary housing erected by their forefathers during the Exodus wanderings. Samples of the fall crop are hung in each family's booth to acknowledge God's faithfulness in providing for His people.

Each day of the Feast of Tabernacles was filled with important festivity. Each day, the high priest of Israel, in a great processional made up of priests and tens of thousands of worshipers, descended from the Temple Mount to pause briefly at the Pool of Siloam. A pitcher was filled with water, and the procession continued via a different route back to the Temple Mount. Here, in the midst of great ceremony, the high priest poured the water out of the pitcher onto the altar. In Israel, the rains normally stop in March, and there is no rain for almost seven months. If God does not provide the "early" rains in October and November, there will be no spring crop, and famine is at the doorstep. This ceremony, then, was intended to invoke God's blessing on the nation so that He might provide life-giving water.

It is in connection with the Feast of Tabernacles that the Gospel of John records a fascinating event. John wrote: "On the last day, that great day of the feast, Jesus stood and cried out, saying, 'If anyone thirsts, let him come to Me and drink. He who believes in Me, as the Scripture has said, out of his heart will flow rivers of living water'" (Jn. 7:37-38). The Son of God was saying in the clearest possible way that He alone was the source of life and blessing — that He could meet every need of the human heart.

The Feast of Tabernacles speaks eloquently of the messianic Kingdom — of a new beginning without the ravages of the curse of sin. In that day, the earth will give her full bounty, all animals will be docile, armies will no longer march, every man will sit under his own fig tree, and righteousness will become a reality in the earth.

Fifteen hundred years before the birth of the Messiah, the seven feasts foretold, in type, the major redemptive works of His life. The four spring feasts related to His first coming: His death was depicted in Passover; that His body would not decay in the grave is seen in Unleavened Bread; His resurrection is illustrated in Firstfruits; and the commencement of the Church and the New Covenant is typified in the Feast of Weeks.

The three fall feasts portray events to be associated with His second coming. The Feast of Trumpets depicts the Rapture of the Church. The Day of Atonement points to a great host of people, Jews and Gentiles, who will be saved when they see Him coming and appropriate the benefits of His death. The Feast of Tabernacles speaks of the day when the Messiah Himself will tabernacle among men, wipe away every tear, and bring in the utopian age or "golden age" of which men have dreamed since time immemorial.

Only a God who is omniscient could have foretold these astounding events. The fool denies His existence; the man of pride refuses to accept His gracious provision of life. Time is running out — the trumpet blast will soon be heard around the world announcing His coming.

זמן

"Then God said, 'Let there be lights in the firmament
of the heavens to divide the day from the night;
and let them be for signs and seasons, and for
days and years'" (Gen. 1:14).

Jewish Time

Kevin L. Howard

A dear friend of mine, with whom I frequently meet, often remarks, "I will be with you in three minutes." I invariably respond with the inquiry, "Is that Jewish time or real time?" Although only spoken in jest, my question really asks, "Will that be a literal three minutes or more like half an hour?"

In a very real sense, "Jewish time," unique as it is, does exist. Months, days, and years are reckoned quite differently from a religious Jewish viewpoint than from that of the rest of the world.

THE JEWISH DAY

For most of the world, a day is based on the Roman reckoning of time which began a new day at midnight. However, in marked contrast, the Jewish day begins at sundown and continues until the next sundown. The basis for this reckoning of time is found in the wording of Scripture. Six times in Genesis 1, the Lord spoke of the day as consisting of "the evening and the morning" (Gen. 1:5, 8, 13, 19, 23, 31). The order of the day was consistent — first the evening (night hours), then the morning (daylight hours). In the Law of Moses, God commanded the Jewish people to keep Yom Kippur from evening to evening (Lev. 23:32). Consequently, Jewish holidays always begin at sundown when the new day begins.

Beginning the day at sundown presents several challenges. The time of sundown continually changes due to the tilting of the earth's axis. Sundown may occur at 5:00 p.m. one Friday night and 4:52 p.m. the next Friday night. Sundown is also dependent upon geographical location. It may occur at 4:34 p.m. in New York City and 5:28 p.m. in Atlanta.

THE JEWISH WEEK

A Time to Rest

Most of the modern world reckons time by a seven-day unit known as a week. The Hebrew word for "week" is derived from the Hebrew word for "seven." The Hebrew days of the week have no specific names but are known as "the first day," "the second day," and so forth. The seventh, however, is known as the "Sabbath" and is set apart from the other six days as a day of rest and worship. All manner of work is prohibited on the Sabbath (sundown Friday to sundown Saturday) by the Law of Moses: "'Work shall be done for six days, but the seventh is the Sabbath of rest, holy to the LORD. Whoever does any work on the Sabbath day, he shall surely be put to death'" (Ex. 31:15).

The Jewish week with its Sabbath finds its origin and meaning in the biblical account of creation (Gen. 1:1-2:3); God created for six days and rested on the seventh. It was not that God was tired; He who is omnipotent cannot grow tired. But God rested in the sense of satisfaction. He saw that what He had created was good and complete, so He rested. To commemorate this, God commanded Moses: "'Therefore the children of Israel shall keep the Sabbath, to observe the Sabbath throughout their generations as a perpetual covenant. It is a sign between Me and the children of Israel forever; for in six days the LORD made the heavens and the earth, and on the seventh day He rested and was refreshed'" (Ex. 31:16-17).

The divine restriction on Sabbath work had a profound impact on ancient Jewish life. Firewood could not be collected (Num. 15:32-36), fires could not be kindled (Ex. 35:3), and travel was restricted (Ex. 16:29). According to later rabbinic tradition, a Sabbath day's journey was defined as no more than 2,000 cubits (a little over one-half mile), or the distance between the ark of God and the people (Josh. 3:4).

The reality of the weekly Sabbath is also deeply etched upon modern Jewish life. In Israeli hotels, a special Sabbath elevator is preprogrammed to stop at every floor at regular intervals on the Sabbath. Pressing an elevator button is considered work and is therefore not allowed. All Jewish bus lines in Jerusalem cease running at sundown Friday and do not resume until Saturday evening. El Al, the official Israeli airline, does not fly on the Sabbath. If a Friday afternoon flight is delayed at the airport for a few hours, it must wait until after the Sabbath before resuming its schedule.

Switching on an electric light is classified as fire-kindling type of work. Therefore, observant Jewish households will usually leave a light burning continuously throughout the Sabbath. Once the Sabbath commences, turning on a light switch is considered work and is forbidden. In the synagogue, a custodian called a "Sabbath Gentile" is usually employed to turn on lights and perform other necessary tasks forbidden under Sabbath work restrictions.

A Time to Rejoice

Sabbath is a special time in the observant Jewish home. Each Friday evening at sundown, the woman of the house will usher in the Sabbath by lighting Sabbath candles (usually two). She will then cover her eyes with her hands and recite the blessing for the candle lighting. Candles are lit on all joyous occasions and holidays, preserving a Jewish tradition that dates back at least to the time of Esther (Est. 8:16).

Later, the father of the house will pour the Sabbath wine and recite the *Kiddush* (Prayer of Sanctification) over the cup of wine. This ancient prayer, from before the time of Christ, offers thanks for the wine and sets it apart unto God.

The Sabbath table is one of beauty. Along with the wine and bright candles, the Sabbath table is adorned with a pure white tablecloth. A mouth-watering fish recipe often serves as the main course, and two delicious loaves of braided *hallah* bread are usually served, covered with a beautifully decorated cloth.

A Time to Reflect

The modern observance of the Sabbath includes a Havdalah ceremony on Saturday evening after sunset. *Havdalah*, from the Hebrew word meaning "separation," serves as a *separation* between the Sabbath holy day and the following days of the secular workweek. During the Havdalah, a cup of wine is filled to overflowing, symbolizing the joy of the Sabbath. As it is held in the right hand, the blessing is recited: "Blessed art Thou, O Lord our God, King of the universe, who creates the fruit of the vine." After the blessing for wine, a blessing is said over an ornate box of aromatic spices. These aromatic spices are then passed around for all to savor as the Sabbath slowly slips away for another week. As the Sabbath draws to a close, a blessing is recited over a festive, double-wick candle which is plaited from a blue and a white candle.

 # THE JEWISH MONTH

Connection to the Moon

 Hebrew months are lunar; that is, they are based upon the appearance of the thin crescent of the new moon. The moon orbits the earth, passing through its phases to the next New Moon, approximately once every 29 $\frac{1}{2}$ days. For this reason, Jewish months generally alternate between 29 or 30 days in length, averaging about 29 $\frac{1}{2}$ days each. Since the Hebrew month is always connected to the New Moon, the Hebrew word for month (*hodesh*) is also the word for "moon."

Biblical Observance

 In biblical times, the beginning of each month was confirmed by the priests and later by the Sanhedrin, Israel's ruling religious body in the time of Jesus. After questioning two reliable witnesses who had seen the New Moon, the council would solemnly declare, "It is sanctified!" In a matter of minutes, word was "telegraphed" from Jerusalem to the large Jewish community in Babylonia. This was accomplished via an elaborate network of signal fires which stretched for hundreds of miles across the Arabian desert.

The first day of every month, known as *Rosh Hodesh* ("the Head of the Month"), was a holy day. Although observed as a day of rest in the time of Amos (Amos 8:5), Rosh Hodesh had no specific work restrictions in the Law of Moses. As such, it was considered a minor holy day.

In the Bible, Rosh Hodesh was marked by special sacrifices (Num. 28:11-15) and the blowing of trumpets (Num. 10:10; Ps. 81:3). These special Rosh Hodesh sacrifices consecrated the new month to the Lord.

The difficulty of visually sighting the New Moon due to clouds led to a two-day celebration of Rosh Hodesh. This seems to be the backdrop for King Saul's concern over David's absence during the first two days of the month (1 Sam. 20:27). Apparently, all members of the royal household and court were required to be at the king's banquet table during Rosh Hodesh.

Modern Observance

Synagogue services on the Sabbath before a New Moon include a special blessing which is recited for the new month. If the Sabbath happens to fall on the last day of the month, one of the readings is taken from 1 Samuel 20 which mentions the New Moon observance in the time of David and Jonathan.

Synagogue services on the day of the New Moon include the recitation of the *Hallel* (praise psalms, specifically Psalms 113-118) and a special reading from the Law which describes the New Moon sacrifices (Num. 28:1-15).

Between the third and fourteenth day of each month, it is also customary to recite a blessing for the New Moon. The *Birkhat HaLevanah* ("Blessing of the Moon") is usually said by Orthodox Jews after the Sabbath *Havdalah* service (Saturday evening) when everyone is joyous and dressed for the occasion. A group will gather outside the synagogue and pronounce the blessing in the open night air while the moon is visible.

Future Observance

In the future messianic Kingdom, it seems clear that King David will be resurrected to reign forever as prince over Israel (Ezek. 37:24-25). He will rank directly under King Messiah who will reign as King over all the earth (Ps. 2:6-8; Zech. 14:9). David's reign will literally fulfill the divine promise to establish his throne forever like the sun and moon (2 Sam. 7:16; Ps.

89:34-37). As the prince, David will be afforded one of the highest honors in the kingdom: that of leading the Sabbath and New Moon worship services before the Lord (Ezek. 46:1-8).

Perhaps it is for this reason that some Jewish prayerbook traditions connect King David with the blessing for the New Moon. In the *Birkat HaLevanah* prayer, it is repeated three times: "*David melech Yisrael chai vekayam*" ("David, King of Israel, lives and is established").[1] King David's connection to the heartfelt cry and yearning for the messianic Kingdom is again felt in the New Moon prayer as the prophet Hosea is quoted: "Afterward the children of Israel shall return and seek the LORD their God and *David their king*"[2] (Hos. 3:5).

The blessing for the New Moon also beseeches God to restore the radiance of the moon to its "pristine fullness as in the seven days of creation." This, too, is a plea for the institution of the messianic Kingdom. The prophet Isaiah prophesied that the day in which the Lord restores the moon to its original brightness will also be the day that "the LORD binds up the bruise of His people, And heals the stroke of their wound" (Isa. 30:26). Israel will repent and be redeemed by the Lord.

Scripture teaches that not only redeemed Israel, but all the righteous of the nations will celebrate the New Moon in the Kingdom: "'And it shall come to pass That from one New Moon to another, And from one Sabbath to another, *All flesh* shall come to worship before Me,' says the LORD" (Isa. 66:23).

Some would teach that there will be neither sun nor moon in the Kingdom and Eternal State. But the Bible actually teaches that "the light of the moon will be as the light of the sun, And the light of the sun will be sevenfold" (Isa. 30:26). The effects of the curse will be lifted. The luminary bodies will be present and restored to their original brilliance, even as the rest of creation is restored to Eden-like conditions during Messiah's reign (Isa. 11:6-9; 51:3; 55:12-13; 65:17-25; Rev. 21:4; 22:3). But their brilliance will be nothing in comparison to that of the Messiah's glory: "Then the moon will be disgraced And the sun ashamed; For the LORD of hosts will reign On Mount Zion . . . gloriously" (Isa. 24:23). "The city [New Jerusalem or Heaven] had no need of the sun or of the moon to shine in it, for the glory of God illuminated it. The Lamb is its light" (Rev. 21:23). The sun and moon will truly be breathtaking with the effects of the curse removed, but in comparison to the Lord's glory, they will be like the light of a candle at noonday. They will no longer provide the primary source of light. In fact, they will blush even to be compared to the radiance of His glory.

THE JEWISH YEAR

Gregorian Calendar

Most of the world today uses a solar calendar which traces its origin to the Roman calendar established under Julius Caesar in 45 B.C. Known as the Julian calendar, it consisted of 365 days each year, and a leap year every fourth year. During a leap year, an extra day was added to the month of February.

With the passage of time, it was noticed that the solar year was actually about 11 minutes shorter than 365 $1/4$ days. An adjustment was needed to compensate for this discrepancy between the solar year and the civil calendar. In 1582, Pope Gregory issued an edict which declared that century years (1600, 1700, etc.) would be leap years, but only if they were also divisible by four hundred (1600, 2000, etc.). This revised Julian calendar was called the Gregorian calendar and is the calendar in use today.

Hebrew Calendar

The Hebrew year reflects a compromise between lunar and solar reckoning. Jewish months are based upon the phases of the moon, with an average length of 29 $1/2$ days. Ordinarily the Jewish year has 12 lunar months or, in other words, about 354 days on the calendar.

The Bible commanded that the various holidays were to be kept in their appointed seasons (Num. 9:2-3). Passover, for example, was to be observed in the springtime. Seasons, however, are determined by the earth's orientation with the sun, not with the moon. If the Hebrew calendar used only a lunar year (354 days), one would be faced with an insurmountable problem. The difference of approximately eleven days between the lunar year (354 days) and the solar year (365 $1/4$ days) would soon cause Passover to be celebrated out of its appointed season in violation of the biblical injunction.

To reconcile this difference, the Jewish calendar is based upon a 19-year cycle in which the third, sixth, eighth, eleventh, fourteenth, seventeenth, and nineteenth years are leap years. During a Jewish leap year, one day is added to the month Adar, and a thirteenth month (29 days), known as *Adar Sheni* ("Second *Adar*"), is added to the calendar. In this sense, the Jewish calendar is a *lunisolar* calendar, a lunar calendar adjusted to the solar seasonal year.

Until A.D. 359, the Sanhedrin presided in Jerusalem as the supreme judicial authority over all Jewish matters. They controlled the formula for determining the New Moon and announced its arrival each month after hearing the testimony of two eyewitnesses. But changing political conditions in the region often hindered timely notification of the start of holidays. This tremendous hardship for those living in the *Diaspora* (Jewish communities outside Israel) threatened the continued observance of holidays. In A.D. 360, Hillel II, the great patriarch, published the Sanhedrin's closely guarded calculations of the Hebrew calendar, thus fixing the present Hebrew calendar and eliminating the need for eyewitnesses. This diminished the Sanhedrin's control over Jewish life and eventually led to their decline.

Because of differences between the Gregorian and Hebrew calendars, Jewish holidays appear to change dates every year. For instance, Passover sometimes occurs in March, at other times in April.

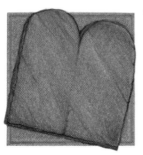

Two Calendars

Few events have shaped the history of Israel as much as the exodus from Egypt. In bringing His people out of Egypt, God's deliverance was so mighty and awesome that the topography of Israel's religious observance was forever altered. Seven holy days were given to Israel by the Lord (Lev. 23). Additionally, Israel was given a new calendar which began its religious New Year in the month of Nisan (March-April), the month in which God delivered Israel out of Egypt. God commanded, "This month shall be your beginning of months; it shall be the first month of the year to you" (Ex. 12:2).

Until the Exodus, Israel had marked her New Year according to the agricultural or civil calendar which began after the harvest. Harvesttime signaled the conclusion of the agricultural year. After harvesttime, the plowing-sowing-reaping cycle began anew. Israel, as an agricultural society, naturally began the New Year after the harvest (Ex. 23:16; 34:22).

After the Exodus, Israel actually observed two New Years — the agricultural and the religious. The religious calendar began its New Year in Nisan (March-April) and was used for all dating in the Bible. However, the more ancient agricultural or civil New Year (September-October, around the Feast of Trumpets) continued to be a tradition within Israel.

The Year of Jubilee was primarily an agricultural holy year which was observed every fiftieth year. During the Year of Jubilee, the land of Israel remained uncultivated for the entire growing season (Lev. 25:11). As such, the Year of Jubilee commenced in the seventh month (Lev. 25:9) of the religious calendar, coinciding with the agricultural New Year in the fall of the year.

With the destruction of the Temple in A.D. 70 and the dispersion of Israel, observance of the Feast of Trumpets (occurring in the seventh month) was diminished. As a result, the Feast of Trumpets came to be celebrated simply as *Rosh Hashanah* ("Head of the Year") since it coincided with the civil New Year. As the modern Jewish New Year, Rosh Hashanah preserves the New Year tradition of the ancient civil calendar.

Israel's recognition of two calendars, one for civil and one for religious purposes, was affirmed by ancient authority. The first-century Jewish historian, Josephus, explained that while Israel was in Egypt they began their calendar in the month Tishri, but "Moses appointed that Nisan . . . should be the first month for their festivals, because he brought them out of Egypt in that month: so that this month began the year as to all the solemnities they observed to the honor of God, although he preserved the original order of the months as to selling and buying, and other ordinary affairs" (*Antiquities of the Jews* 1. 3.3). The ancient rabbinical voice from before the time of Jesus commented, "In the month that the ancient ones called the first month . . . but now it is called the seventh month" (Targum Jonathan on 1 Ki. 8:2).

Biblical Calendar

The biblical year consisted of 360 days or twelve months of 30 days each. In the account of the Flood, Noah's ark was in the waters for five months (Gen. 7:11; 8:4) which were equivalent to 150 days (Gen. 7:24; 8:3). In the Book of Revelation, $3^{1}/_{2}$ years (Rev. 12:14) were equivalent to forty-two months (Rev. 11:2; 13:5) which were equivalent to 1,260 days (Rev. 11:3; 12:6). In each instance, the month was viewed as thirty days and the year as 360 days. The exact details of how that calendar was periodically adjusted to keep it in alignment with the solar year have been lost.

Hebrew Months

The names of the Hebrew months were originally Canaanite, borrowed from the inhabitants of the land of Israel in the days of the patriarchs. The first month was called Abib (Ex. 13:4; 23:15; 34:18; Dt. 16:1); the second month, Ziv (1 Ki. 6:1, 37); the seventh month, Ethanim (1 Ki. 8:2); and the eighth month, Bul (1 Ki. 6:38). After the Babylonian captivity (586 B.C.), the Babylonian names of the months were adopted and continue in use today.

Dating System

Much of the world uses the dating system which reckons years before the birth of Jesus (B.C., "Before Christ") and since His birth (A.D., *Anno Domini*, Latin for "In the Year of Our Lord"). Because most Jewish people do not accept the messiahship of Jesus, the same time periods are referred to in Jewish circles as "Before Common Era" (B.C.E.) and "Common Era" (C.E.).

The Jewish dating system used today actually reckons time from the traditional year of the creation of the world (Fall, 3761 B.C.). Therefore, the current Hebrew year can be calculated by adding 3760 or 3761 to the Gregorian year (because the Jewish New Year begins in September/October, and the Gregorian New Year in January). For example, A.D. 2000 + 3760/3761 = 5760/5761.

Israel's Feasts

Israel's feasts are infinitely more important than just a series of cultural observances. These feasts are appointed by the Lord, and they are *owned* by the Lord. He calls them *my* feasts (Lev. 23:2).

The feasts of Leviticus 23 are also more than feasts in the sense of special foods or festive occasions. Many have no food at all connected to them, and some are very somber in tone. The Hebrew word *moed* has more of the meaning of a "solemn appointed time." These "feasts" in actuality are "appointments" or "set times" with the Lord. Some are appointed days, and some are appointed weeks. Collectively, the "feasts" of the Lord form the divine appointment calendar, with Jerusalem as the meeting place (Isa. 33:20).

The Jewish Calendar

MONTH	LENGTH	DATE	HOLIDAY
1. Nisan	30 days	Nisan 14 Nisan 15-21 Nisan 16	Passover Unleavened Bread Firstfruits
2. Iyar	29 days		
3. Sivan	30 days	Sivan 6	Shavuot (Weeks)
4. Tammuz	29 days		
5. Av	30 days	Av 9	Tisha B'Av
6. Elul	29 days		
7. Tishri	30 days	Tishri 1 Tishri 10 Tishri 15-21	Rosh Hashanah Yom Kippur Sukkot (Tabernacles)
8. Heshvan	29 or 30 days		
9. Kislev	29 or 30 days	Kislev 25-Tevet 2/3	Hanukkah
10. Tevet	29 days		
11. Shevat	30 days		
12. Adar	29 days (30 in leap year)	Adar 14	Purim

The Feasts of the Lord

FEAST	DATE	SIGNIFICANCE
PASSOVER	*Nisan 14* *Spring*	*Passover speaks of redemption. Messiah, the Passover Lamb, would be sacrificed for us.*
UNLEAVENED BREAD	*Nisan 15-21* *Spring*	*Unleavened Bread speaks of sanctification. Messiah's body would not decay in the grave.*
FIRSTFRUITS	*Nisan 16* *Spring*	*Firstfruits speaks of resurrection. Messiah would rise triumphantly from the grave on the third day.*
WEEKS	*50 days after Firstfruits* *Spring*	*Weeks/Shavuot speaks of origination. Messiah would send the Holy Spirit to inaugurate the New Covenant and Church Age.*
TRUMPETS	*Tishri 1* *Fall*	*Trumpets/Rosh Hashanah points to the future day when the Messiah returns to rescue the righteous (Rapture) and judge the wicked.*
YOM KIPPUR	*Tishri 10* *Fall*	*Yom Kippur/Day of Atonement points to the future day when Israel repents of her sins and turns to the Messiah for salvation.*
TABERNACLES	*Tishri 15-21* *Fall*	*Tabernacles/Sukkot points to the future day when the Messiah sets up the messianic Kingdom and tabernacles among men.*

THE APPLICATION

Many people erroneously equate the keeping of holy days with righteousness before God. Some slip into synagogue for Yom Kippur, others slip into church for Christmas and Easter. They would like to believe that they are righteous in God's eyes for doing their religious "duty."

God rebuked Israel for keeping the *external requirements* of the Law while disregarding a *heart relationship* with Him: "The New Moons, the Sabbaths, and the calling of assemblies — I cannot endure iniquity and the sacred meeting. Your New Moons and your appointed feasts My soul hates; They are a trouble to Me, I am weary of bearing them" (Isa. 1:13-14; cf. Amos 5:21).

But why would God hate the feast days when it was He who had instituted them? Obviously, He did not hate the feast days themselves but the hypocritical manner in which they were kept. The people had misunderstood and distorted God's law. They had abandoned a personal relationship with God. Instead, they sought after self-righteousness through keeping the requirements of the Law.

The outward *requirements* of the Law were meaningless without an inward *relationship* with the living God. It was for this reason that God commanded Israel: "Hear, O Israel: The LORD our God, the LORD is one! You shall love the LORD your God with all your *heart*, with all your *soul*, and with all your *strength*. And these words which I command you today, shall be in your heart" (Dt. 6:4-6). So supreme in importance are these words that they begin the *Shema*, the most holy prayer within Judaism. They are also written on the doorposts of all observant Jews and in the *tefillin* (Scripture boxes or phylacteries) worn on the forehead and forearm during prayer.

The Messiah also underscored this truth: "'You shall love the LORD your God with all your heart, with all your soul, and with all your mind.' This is the first and great commandment" (Mt. 22:37-38). First and foremost, God desires a heart relationship.

Many in Isaiah's day believed they were righteous before God because they were religious — they followed the *mitzvot* (commandments), they prayed, they kept the holy days. Today, the overwhelming majority of mankind, whether Jewish or Gentile, find themselves in an identical situation. They mistakenly believe that keeping a list of religious rites or holidays will gain them acceptance in God's sight.

The Bible likens the feast days to shadows which prophetically point to the person and work of history's most stellar individual — the Messiah of

Israel (Col. 2:16-17). Together these feasts outline the work of the Messiah from Calvary to the messianic Kingdom. He alone is the source and substance, whereas the holy days are merely the shadows cast by His indelible mark on history.

This can be illustrated by a husband who returns home after a long trip. His heart may beat faster in anticipation, seeing the outline of his wife's shadow as she comes to the front door, but he does not embrace her shadow. There would be no satisfaction in that. Instead, he steps through the doorway and embraces her in person, rather than her shadow.

Jesus proclaimed, "I am the way, the truth, and the life. No one comes to the Father except through me" (Jn. 14:6). Are you chasing shadows, or have you fully embraced the Messiah? Only He can save.

 NOTES

[1] De Sola Pool, David, *The Traditional Prayer Book for Sabbath and Festivals* (New Hyde Park: University Books, 1960), p. 462.

[2] *Ibid.*, p. 464.

פֶּסַח

"'On the fourteenth day of the first month at twilight is the LORD's Passover'" (Lev. 23:5).

Passover

Kevin L. Howard

Passover is an ancient feast, one that spans some thirty-five centuries of human existence. Set in the time of Egypt's great pyramids, the Passover story is impassioned by fiery accounts of: a death sentence for Jewish infants; a baby floating in a river; Jewish slaves; a burning bush; Egyptian sorcerers; tense confrontations with the Pharaoh; divine plagues; a pursuing army; the parting of a sea; and the birth of a nation at the foot of a thundering wilderness mountain.

Passover carries a powerful message for today. This holiday forms the primary background for understanding the events of the Upper Room, the symbolism of the Lord's Table, and the meaning of the Messiah's death.

THE BIBLICAL OBSERVANCE

The Meaning of Passover

For more than 400 years, the Jewish people had lived in Egypt (Ex. 12:40). The time had come for God to bring them back to their land as He had promised (Gen. 46:3-4; 50:24). In Exodus 11, God detailed, through His servant Moses, the tenth and final judgment plague which would befall the Egyptians and their false gods. At midnight, the Lord would pass through the land and kill the firstborn of each family and of all the cattle. With this final, climactic plague, God would dramatically free His people from the bondage of Egypt.

In Exodus 12, God outlined explicit steps to be taken by those who trusted in Him so that they, unlike Pharaoh and the Egyptians, would not be struck down by the final plague. They were to select a year-old male lamb in its prime. It was to be a perfect lamb without any flaw or defect. It was to be taken out from the flock on the tenth day of the Hebrew month of Nisan and kept until the fourteenth day of the month. This would allow time for each family to observe the lamb and confirm that it was fit. This would also allow time for each family to become personally attached to their lamb so that it would no longer be just *a lamb* (Ex. 12:3), but *their lamb* (Ex. 12:5). This would deeply impress upon them the costly nature of the sacrifice. An innocent one was to die in their place.

On the evening of the fourteenth, as the warm afternoon sun was setting, the lambs were to be publicly killed by "the whole assembly." All the people were to be responsible for the death of the lambs. Yet, in contrast, each family was to individually apply the blood of their lamb to the doorposts of their own home as a visible sign of their faith in the Lord (Ex. 12:13). At that moment, the innocent lamb became their substitute making it possible for the Lord's judgment to "pass over" them. And so the Lord instituted Passover as "a night of solemn observance to the LORD for bringing them out of the land of Egypt" (Ex. 12:42).

The Time of Passover

By biblical definition, Passover is a one-day feast that is immediately followed by the seven-day Feast of Unleavened Bread. Both feasts today are usually blurred together as a single entity and simply called "Passover."

God ordained that Passover be observed each year on the fourteenth day of the Hebrew month, Nisan (March-April), the day that God delivered His people from Egypt (Ex. 12:6; Lev. 23:5; Num. 9:3; 28:16). His deliverance was so mighty and awesome that Israel's religious calendar was forever altered. In commemoration of this miraculous deliverance, the month of Nisan (known as Abib before the Babylonian captivity, Ex. 13:4; 34:18) became the first month of the Hebrew religious year from that time forward (Ex. 12:2; Num. 9:5; 28:16).

The Record of Passover

By all biblical accounts, the lamb was the core requisite for Passover (Ex. 12; 34:25; Dt. 16:1-7). It was the centerpiece of all that was accomplished. If there was no lamb, there would be no deliverance. So central was the lamb to Passover observance that the term "the Passover" came to be used interchangeably of the lamb as well as the holiday (Ex. 12:21; Dt. 16:2, 6; cf. Lk. 22:7; 1 Cor. 5:7). One could not exist without the other. The lamb embodied the holiday, and without it, the holiday was meaningless.

In all, God required three symbolic foods to be eaten that Passover night — the lamb, matzah (unleavened bread), and bitter herbs (Ex. 12:8). The sacrifice was to be a young lamb, depicting innocence. It was to be roasted with fire portraying the judgment that would befall it instead of the firstborn. Matzah (unleavened bread) was to be eaten symbolizing the purity of the sacrifice since leaven, with its souring characteristic, was often a symbol of sin (1 Cor. 5:6-8). Bitter herbs were to be eaten as a reminder of the suffering of the lamb.

The Importance of Passover

Several important facts must be understood regarding the observance of Passover. There was only one Passover when the Lord passed through the land in judgment. Every observance since then has been a memorial commemorating that occasion (Ex. 13:3).

Passover holds great distinction among the religious feasts of the world. Passover is the oldest continuously observed feast in existence today, celebrated for some 3,500 years. Passover was celebrated in the Sinai wilderness one year after Israel left Egypt (Num. 9:1-14); it was celebrated as the Jewish people came into the land of Israel (Josh. 5:10-12); it was celebrated in the days of King Hezekiah (2 Chr. 30) and King Josiah (2 Ki. 23:21-23; 2 Chr. 35:1-19); it was celebrated after the return from Babylonian captivity (Ezra 6:19-20); and Passover was celebrated extensively in the days of Jesus (Jn. 11:55). Even today, more Jewish people keep Passover than any of the other Jewish holy days. It is a strong, cohesive force within the fabric of Jewish culture and community.

The observance of Passover was so important that God graciously gave an alternate date for those who were unable to observe Passover on Nisan 14. Those who had become defiled by touching a dead body or were away on a long journey could celebrate Passover thirty days later on the fourteenth of the second month (Num. 9:1-14; cf. 2 Chr. 30:2, 15). None of the other divinely appointed feasts had this accommodation.

The Service of Passover

God commanded that Passover be observed as a memorial forever (Ex. 12:14). He also declared that it was to be kept by a service (Ex. 12:25). This service was to incorporate the lamb, matzah (unleavened bread), and bitter herbs and to raise questions in the minds of the children so that the Exodus story could be rehearsed from generation to generation (Ex.

A PILLOW is placed near the left arm of the leader on which to recline during the Seder. The custom of reclining while eating is of ancient Persian origin. It symbolizes freedom, since slaves were never permitted to recline in leisure at a meal.

HAZERET is a whole bitter herb such as horseradish, radish, or onion. It is in addition to the maror since the biblical command in Numbers 9:11 is to eat the meal with bitter herbs (plural).

The ROASTED EGG in some traditions represents the required peace offering in the Temple for the second day of Passover.

SALT WATER symbolizes the Jewish tears shed during Egyptian bondage and God's miraculous parting of the Red Sea.

The HAGGADAH (Heb. "the telling") is so named from the Lord's command to "tell your son" (Ex. 13:8). It is the book which relates the Passover story through readings, songs, and prayers in the traditional prescribed order.

The KIPPA (Hebrew) or YARMULKE (Yiddish) is the small head covering worn by Jewish males to show reverence for God. There is no command for such a practice in Scripture, but it arose by tradition in postbiblical times.

HAROSET is a sweet mixture of finely chopped apple, nuts, cinnamon, and wine made to resemble the red-brown clay and mortar used by Israel in making the bricks of Pharaoh's pyramids. Its sweetness is a reminder of the sweetness of God's redemption from slavery.

The SEDER TRAY is tray or platter which usually has six circul indentations so that t symbolic Passover foods may be individ ally displayed. It is th central item on the modern Passover ta

The **SHANKBONE** of a lamb is a stark reminder of the Passover lamb sacrificed each year in the days of the Temple. The sacrificial system ceased with the Roman destruction of the Temple in A.D. 70.

MAROR (bitter herbs), usually ground horseradish, is a mandatory item for Passover. It is a reminder of the bitterness which the Israelites suffered as slaves in Egypt.

KARPAS, usually parsley, bitter lettuce, or watercress, is considered a bitter herb. Its green color is a reminder of the springtime during which Passover occurs and also of the hyssop plant used to apply the blood to the doorposts.

ELIJAH'S CUP is the extra cup of wine poured in the hope that the prophet Elijah might come and announce the arrival of the Messiah. Rabbinic tradition holds that the Messiah will come during Passover, the season of redemption, to bring about the final redemption from dispersion. However, according to Malachi 4:5, Elijah must appear first.

WINE is a symbol of joy. Rabbinic law commands that four cups of wine be taken during the Seder to symbolize the fourfold expression of the Lord's promised deliverance (Ex. 6:6-7). According to rabbinic law, this wine must be red.

CANDLES are lit at sunset and a prayer pronounced over them by the mother of the house to begin the Passover service. The candles, with their bright, warm glow, symbolize the solemnity of the occasion and set Passover apart as a special day.

THREE MATZAHS (unleavened bread) are placed on the Passover table with one in each pocket of the embroidered matzah *tash* (linen bag). Some rabbinic authorities suggest that the three matzahs represent the three groups of Jewish people: the priests, the Levites, and the Israelites. However, there is no biblical basis for this explanation.

12:26-27). The Lord, however, did not detail the order of the service, only that it was to be kept.

Several centuries before Christ, a somewhat traditionalized Passover service began to emerge. This ritual Passover service was called the *Seder* (pronounced SAY-der) from the Hebrew word meaning "order." It prescribed the traditional order of the Scripture readings, prayers, symbolic foods, and songs in the Passover service. The basic order of the Passover Seder today remains much as it was 2,000 years ago even though the service continued to be embellished with more songs and traditions up through the Middle Ages.

THE MODERN OBSERVANCE

The Passover Seder

Before the arrival of Passover, painstaking preparation takes place within the Jewish home to rid it of all leavened bread and related products. Houses are scrubbed, pockets are turned inside out and laundered, cooking utensils are scalded, and everyday dinnerware and flatware are replaced with the finest Passover china, silver, and crystal.

The Passover service itself is usually quite lengthy as the Passover story unfolds through the many prayers, songs, and narrative readings in the *Haggadah*. The Seder sometimes lasts until midnight or even the early hours of the morning before tired family members wander off to bed.

As the family is seated, special seating arrangements are observed. The leader sits at the head of the festive dinner table. The youngest sits at his right side in order to fulfill a special role later in the Seder service. To the left of the leader, the guest of honor is seated, or sometimes the place setting is reserved for the prophet Elijah.

The mother of the house ushers in the holiday by lighting the Passover candles. She then covers her eyes with her hands and recites a Hebrew blessing over the candles thanking God for the special occasion: "Blessed art Thou, O Lord our God, King of the Universe, Who has set us apart by His Word, and in whose Name we light the festival lights."

The First Cup

The Lord used four expressions to describe His promised deliverance from Egypt: "I will bring you out"; "I will rescue you from their bondage"; "I will redeem you"; and "I will take you as My people" (Ex. 6:6-7). Since wine is often a symbol of the joy of harvest, four cups of wine are taken during the Passover service to reflect the fourfold joy of the Lord's redemption.

To begin the service, the father pours the first cup of wine and asks everyone to rise from the table. The father then lifts his cup toward heaven and recites the *Kiddush* ("prayer of sanctification") to set the day apart to God:

> Blessed art Thou, O Lord our God, King of the universe, Who createst the fruit of the vine. Blessed art Thou, O Lord our God, Who hast chosen us for Thy service from among the nations. . . . Blessed art Thou, O Lord our God, King of the universe, Who hast kept us in life, Who hast preserved us, and hast enabled us to reach this season.

It was the Messiah, as the leader of the Seder service observed in the Upper Room, who said the Kiddush. "Then He took the cup, and gave thanks" (Lk. 22:17).

The Washing of the Hands

The second ceremony of the Seder is known as the "washing of the hands." One of the family members brings a pitcher of water, bowl, and towel to each person at the table to wash his hands. The ceremony is a symbolic act of purification as they prepare to handle the food.

It was probably this ceremony in the Seder that the Messiah used to teach His disciples an object lesson. "[Jesus] rose from supper and laid aside His garments, took a towel and girded Himself. After that, He poured water into a basin and began to wash the disciples' feet, and to wipe them with the towel with which He was girded" (Jn. 13:4-5). His object lesson demonstrated that He was about to become the suffering Servant of the Lord, and as such, He would be the One to cleanse them.

The Green Vegetable

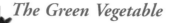

After the hands are washed, the *karpas* (green vegetable) is dipped into the salt water and eaten. The green vegetable is a reminder that Passover occurs in the springtime. The salt water is a reminder of the tears of pain and suffering shed by the Jewish people in slavery.

The Middle Matzah

Next, the leader removes the middle matzah from the linen bag to break it in half. Half is replaced, and half is carefully wrapped in a linen napkin and hidden away in the house while the children cover their eyes. It reappears later in the service to illustrate a very important truth.

The Four Questions

At this point, the youngest child is called on to recite his diligently rehearsed part. The child asks the traditional Passover questions to fulfill Exodus 12:26: "When your children say to you, 'What do you mean by this service?'" Beaming with joy and accomplishment the child will ask:

Why is this night different from all other nights? On all other nights, we eat either leavened or unleavened bread, but on this night, only unleavened bread? On all other nights, we eat all kinds of herbs, but on this night, only bitter herbs? On all other nights, we do not dip even once, but on this night, we dip twice? On all other nights, we eat either sitting or reclining, but on this night, we eat reclining?

Often the youngest will recline upon the leader. This was the context of the apostle John reclining upon Jesus at their Passover supper. John recorded, "Now there was leaning on Jesus' bosom one of His disciples, whom Jesus loved" (Jn. 13:23). This would indicate that John sat to the right of the

Savior and was the youngest at the meal, a position consistent with early Church tradition that John was the youngest apostle. John would have had the honor of asking the questions that night.

The Second Cup

Next, the second cup of wine is poured, and in response to the four questions, a lengthy narrative recounting the Passover story begins. The story relates the whole panorama of the beginnings of the nation: the calling of Abraham in Ur; God's promises to the patriarchs; the story of Joseph and his brothers; the enslavement of the Jewish nation; the deliverance brought at the hand of Moses; and the giving of the Law at Sinai.

As the ten plagues are described, a tiny bit of wine is poured out for each plague. This expresses the sorrow felt for the suffering of the Egyptians. As the Passover story unfolds, the Seder tray and its symbolic elements are carefully explained and woven into the telling of the Passover story.

Before the second cup of wine is taken, the first half of the praise psalms, known in Judaism as the *Hallel* (Ps. 113-118), is recited responsively. *Hallel* is a Hebrew word meaning "praise." This word has made its way into many languages in the form of *halleluyah*, meaning "praise Jehovah." According to the Talmud, which records the ancient rabbinic commentary on Jewish practice, the Levites would chant this group of psalms while the Passover lambs for each family were being sacrificed.

The Dipping of the Matzah

In preparation for the meal, everyone present washes his hands a second time for ceremonial cleansing.

Then the upper matzah and the remainder of the middle matzah are broken into pieces and distributed to everyone. Each person must eat a piece of matzah dipped in the horseradish and *haroset* (apple mixture). This is a reminder of the sweetness of God's redemption in the midst of their bitter slavery.

Each person then puts a filling of horseradish between two pieces of the matzah. This is called the "Hillel Sandwich." It is named in honor of the brilliant and revered first-century rabbi who taught that enough of the bitter herb should be taken to bring tears to the eyes. In this way, each participant can personally identify with his forefathers who were slaves in Egypt.

It was this ritual which gave rise to another important event in the Last Supper. The Messiah foretold that one of the disciples would betray Him (Jn. 13:21-27). Peter motioned to John who was reclining against Jesus to inquire of whom this was spoken. Jesus replied that it would be the one to whom He gave a dipped sop (broken piece of matzah). Jesus dipped the matzah and gave it to Judas Iscariot.

The Scripture is not specific as to the seating arrangement. It could be that Judas was sitting to the left of the Lord in the seat of honor and quite naturally would have received the matzah first according to tradition. It could also be that Jesus reached across the circle to begin with Judas first. However, if tradition was kept, everyone received a dipped piece of matzah that night. Perhaps this is why the disciples were still not clear as to who would be the betrayer. In either case, Judas left the service and went out to finalize the betrayal. This ceremony occurred before the meal, and Judas was not present later when Jesus instituted Communion after the dinner.

The Dinner

Next, the dinner is served. In the day of Jesus, it would have consisted of roasted lamb, served with bitter herbs and matzah. Today, however, the meal is far more varied and sumptuous. A traditional Passover meal may include delicious Jewish dishes of gefilte fish, matzah ball soup, glazed chicken, matzah nut stuffing, potato kugel, honeyed carrots, stewed fruit, and sponge cake. In every way it is a meal fit for a king!

The Afikomen

After the meal, the children are sent out to find the broken half-matzah that was wrapped and hidden away. It is known as the *afikomen*. The children search high and low with great excitement for they know that the one who finds it will receive a reward. From a remote corner of the house, shouts of delight announce that the desired treasure has been discovered. Rabbinic law requires that a small piece of the *afikomen* be broken off and eaten by everyone present at the service as a reminder of the Passover lamb.

The Third Cup

Next in the ceremony, the third cup of wine, called the *Cup of Redemption*, is poured and sipped.

It was here in the Passover Seder that the Messiah instituted the Lord's table. Luke reveals that it was "the cup after supper" (Lk. 22:20), the third cup or *Cup of Redemption*, that Jesus chose to be a reminder of His work on the cross.

Passover is closely associated with the fervent hope for the coming of the Messiah. After the third cup, a child is sent to the front door to hopefully welcome in the prophet Elijah. It is hoped that the prophet will step through the doorway, drink his cup of wine, and announce the coming of the Messiah. This tradition is actually rooted in the Hebrew Scriptures, for Malachi prophesied, "I will send you Elijah the prophet Before the coming of the great and dreadful day of the LORD" (Mal. 4:5).

Many believe that Elijah will be one of the two messianic witnesses mentioned in Revelation 11 since one of them will perform the miracles of Elijah. Although the Scripture teaches that Elijah will return in the future, it does not name the two witnesses, and one cannot be absolutely dogmatic about their identification.

The Fourth Cup

The fourth cup of wine, called the *Cup of Acceptance*, or *Praise*, is poured and taken. It was this cup that the Messiah said He would not drink until He drank it with the disciples in the Kingdom (Mt. 26:29). He knew that the hour of His acceptance by His Jewish nation was yet future, and therefore His joy would not be full until then.

Closing Hymn

At the conclusion of the service, a hymn is usually sung or recited. This was also the tradition in the day of Jesus. Matthew states, "And when they had sung a hymn, they went out" (Mt. 26:30). Perhaps since Matthew was writing to a Jewish audience, he knew that they would know the name of the hymn since, by tradition, every Seder ends with the latter half of the *Hallel* (Ps. 115-118).

How ironic that just hours before Jesus was betrayed and went to the cross, He sang the prophetic words of Psalm 118: "The stone which the builders rejected Has become the chief cornerstone. This was the LORD's doing; It is marvelous in our eyes. This is the day the LORD has made; We will rejoice and be glad in it. Save now, I pray, O LORD; O LORD, I pray, send now prosperity. Blessed is he who comes in the name of the LORD!" (Ps. 118:22-26). The Messiah sang these words just hours before He fulfilled them in becoming the stone that was rejected by the religious leaders (cf. Mt. 21:42; Mk. 12:10; Acts 4:11).

How utterly tragic that the majority of the Jewish nation did not realize the truth of this Psalm, that the Messiah would first be rejected and suffer before He would reign on David's throne. How doubly tragic, since Psalm 118 was generally viewed as messianic and was even sung to Jesus proclaiming Him the Messiah at His so-called triumphal entry. Matthew recorded: "Then the multitudes who went before and those who followed cried out, saying: 'Hosanna [Hebrew for "Save now"] to the Son of David [a messianic title]! Blessed is He who comes in the name of the LORD!'" (Mt. 21:9).

◼ ▰▰▰▰ THE FULFILLMENT

Since the entire Passover service is woven with rich symbolism, it must be asked: "Why three matzahs?" One rabbinic tradition holds that they represent the three groups of Jewish people: the priests, the Levites, and the Israelites. Another tradition holds that they represent the three patriarchs: Abraham, Isaac, and Jacob. Yet rabbinic tradition is at a loss to explain why the middle matzah must be broken. Why must the Levites be broken and not the other groups? Or, why must Isaac be broken and not Abraham nor Jacob? Rabbinic tradition is silent on such an important issue.

Neither explanation fits the symbolism behind this *breaking* ceremony. In reality, the triunity of the Godhead is being symbolized — three persons within the oneness of God, just as three matzahs are in the oneness of the linen bag. The second person of the Godhead, the Son, came to earth as the Messiah. He was broken (died), wrapped, and hidden away (buried), and brought back at the third cup of wine (resurrected the third day).

At first glance, this assertion may appear to be a fanciful attempt to Christianize the Jewish Passover, but the evidence overwhelmingly argues to the contrary. First, the *afikomen* was not present in the day of Jesus. It was a later addition to the Passover. The last solid food taken in that day was the lamb at the dinner. Rabbinic tradition holds that the *afikomen* now represents the lamb, and therefore everyone *must eat* of it.

Second, there is much debate among the rabbis concerning the meaning of the word *afikomen*. The problem is compounded since *afikomen* does not exist in the Hebrew language. It is just not there! Rabbinic concensus usually explains that it means *dessert* since it is eaten after the meal where the dessert would normally be eaten. Amazingly, *afikomen* is the only Greek word (the common language of Jesus' day) in the Passover Seder. Everything else is Hebrew. It is the second aorist form of the Greek verb *ikneomai*. The translation is electrifying. It simply means — *I came.*

Many traditions have developed around the *afikomen*. Moroccan Jews save a piece of the *afikomen* for use when traveling at sea throughout the year. They believe that if a piece of the *afikomen* is tossed into the stormy waves, it will still the waters. It is easy to see the origin of this tradition as Jesus spoke and calmed the stormy Sea of Galilee.

It must be asked, "How could the *afikomen*, if it speaks of Jesus, make its way into the Jewish Passover when the majority of Jewish people today do not accept Jesus as the Messiah?" The situation in the first century must be examined to shed light on this question.

At the Feast of Weeks (also known as *Shavuot* or "Pentecost") in Acts 2, three thousand sons of Israel from many different countries believed on the Lord. The total count was actually much higher since the three thousand did not include the women or children. These Jewish believers would have taken the message of the Savior with them to their Jewish brethren as they returned to their homelands. Many undoubtedly came to the Lord as a result of their testimony. In Acts 21:20, James and all the elders told Paul, "You see, brother, how many myriads of Jews there are who have believed." They were talking only about Jewish believers in Jerusalem and numbered them in the thousands. Some estimate that by the end of the first century there were one million Jewish believers in the Messiah. While this was certainly not a majority within the nation, it was a large enough number to send shock waves throughout synagogues everywhere concerning the messiahship of Jesus.

Another first-century event not only set the stage but mandated a change in the Passover observance. The Roman war machine rolled into Israel and, in A.D. 70, leveled the breathtaking Temple. This was a disaster of the highest magnitude since the majority of the Levitical law was based upon the Temple and its sacrifices. Without the Temple, there could be no more sacrifices. Without the sacrifices, there could be no more Passover lamb, for the Lord had strictly commanded, "Therefore you shall sacrifice the

Passover to the LORD your God, from the flock and the herd, in the place where the LORD chooses to put His name" (Dt. 16:2). Without the Passover lamb, the future of Passover observance was threatened. The Jewish people faced the dilemma of ceasing to observe Passover or changing it to be observed without a lamb.

In addition, Jewish believers had already broken away from the sacrificial system, believing that the Messiah had made a once-and-for-all sacrifice upon the cross. They were already celebrating Passover without the lamb, choosing to incorporate the broken matzah (*afikomen*) into the service at the precise point at which the Lord had said, "This do in remembrance of me." It is not difficult to imagine this tradition being borrowed by others seeking to switch to a "lambless" Passover without their even realizing the full significance behind the ceremony.

Ultimately, Passover foreshadowed the Jewish Messiah as the true Passover Lamb. The Hebrew prophet Isaiah spoke of the Messiah in terms of the Passover lamb and of the greater redemption that He would bring (Isaiah 53). He would be the innocent, pure Lamb upon whom the judgment of God would fall in place of the people. He would be the One who, with great bitterness of suffering and death, would shed His blood to provide the greater deliverance from sin.

How tragic that in millions of Jewish homes today the most obscure ceremony in the Passover (the *afikomen*) is the one that gives it its greatest and most powerful meaning. The *afikomen* (the "He came") has been an annual reminder that the Messiah, the true Passover Lamb, has already come.

And so, year after year, the small voices of children drift through the night: "Why is this night different?" And the testimony of the *afikomen* echoes back in reply, "I came," for it was on this holiday that the true Passover Lamb was crucified, buried, and on the third day rose again to provide the greater redemption, the deliverance from sin. It is only in Him that the Passover message finds its fullness. The Lamb still cannot be separated from the holiday.

There is no question that Jesus is *the* Passover Lamb. Scripture records it. History echoes it. Yet one final Passover question remains, and it is the most important of all: "Is He *your* Passover Lamb — have you placed your trust in the Messiah and His sacrifice as your only hope of Heaven?" Even as the ancient Israelite was required to individually apply the blood to his door, so, too, today men and women must individually make a decision concerning the Lamb of God. There is still no deliverance without the Lamb.

הג המצות

" 'And on the fifteenth day of the same month is the Feast of Unleavened Bread to the LORD; seven days you must eat unleavened bread' " (Lev. 23:6).

The Feast of Unleavened Bread

Kevin L. Howard

Israel's second feast is named after the bread which is required to be eaten during the holiday. The Hebrew Scriptures call this feast *Hag Hamatzot*. *Matzah* and the plural *matzot* are the Hebrew words for "unleavened bread." Therefore, this holiday is known as the Feast of Unleavened Bread. An understanding of the practical truth taught by this important feast is absolutely vital for godly living today.

◼ THE BIBLICAL OBSERVANCE

The Meaning of the Feast

The Feast of Unleavened Bread is a reminder of God's miraculous deliverance from Egyptian bondage, for when Israel fled from Egypt in the middle of the night, there was no time for bread dough to rise. So the Lord commanded, "Seven days you shall eat unleavened bread with it, that is, the bread of affliction (for you came out of the land of Egypt in haste), that you may remember the day in which you came out of the land of Egypt all the days of your life" (Dt. 16:3; cf. Ex. 12:39).

The Time of the Feast

The Feast of Unleavened Bread is observed in the early spring (March–April). It begins on the 15th day of the Hebrew month of Nisan and lasts for seven days. Because the Feast of Unleavened Bread (a seven-day holiday) begins the day after Passover (a one-day holiday), often the two holidays are blurred together and collectively referred to as "the eight days of Passover." In the days of the Second Temple (in Jesus' time), it was also common to call all eight days the Feast of Unleavened Bread (Lk. 22:1, 7).

The Importance of the Feast

The Feast of Unleavened Bread was a prominent biblical feast. Unlike the other feasts which were instituted in Leviticus 23, the commandment instituting this feast was given prior to the Exodus from Egypt (Ex. 12:14-20). Passover and the Feast of Unleavened Bread were instituted first. The details for the other feasts came later. The Feast of Unleavened Bread was also the first of the three annual pilgrim feasts. During three of the seven annual feasts (the feasts of Unleavened Bread, Weeks, and Tabernacles), all Jewish men were required to present themselves before the Lord at the Temple (Ex. 23:14-17; 34:18-23; Dt. 16:16; 2 Chr. 8:13).

In keeping this commandment, the Messiah journeyed to Jerusalem for each pilgrim feast. After one such pilgrimage for the Feast of Unleavened Bread at age twelve, the Messiah had a fascinating encounter. It is recorded: "And when He was twelve years old, they went up to Jerusalem according to *the custom of the feast.* When they had finished the days, as they returned, the Boy Jesus lingered behind in Jerusalem. . . . Now so it was that after three days they found Him in the temple, sitting in the midst of the teachers [experts in the Scriptures], both listening to them and asking them questions. And all who heard Him were astonished at His understanding and answers" (Lk. 2:42-43, 46-47). The Messiah utterly amazed Israel's finest Torah scholars. He was a lowly Galilean, He had no university training, and He was only twelve years old, not even of *Bar Mitzvah* age (age 13). Yet, His understanding and comprehension of Scripture were staggering. Never before had they met one like this.

The Record of the Feast

The biblical record gives only three instructions for the Feast of Unleavened Bread. Special sacrifices were to be offered in the Temple each day of the feast (Lev. 23:8; Num. 28:19-24). The first and seventh days of the feast were sabbaths with prohibitions on all work (Ex. 12:16; Lev. 23:7-8; Num. 28:25; Dt. 16:8), and leaven was strictly forbidden. No less than six passages emphasize the prohibition of leaven during this feast (Ex. 12:14-20; 13:6-8; 23:15; 34:18; Lev. 23:6; Dt. 16:3, 8).

In Hebrew, leaven is known as *hametz,* which literally means "sour." Leaven (usually yeast or baking powder) is used to produce fermentation, especially in bread dough. As leaven sours the dough, tiny gas bubbles are produced which cause the dough to rise.

Not only is the eating of leavened foods (such as bread and rolls) forbidden during the feast, but even the presence of leaven within one's house is unlawful. The Lord commanded Moses, "Seven days you shall eat unleavened bread. On the first day you shall remove leaven *from your houses*. For whoever eats leavened bread from the first day until the seventh day, that person shall be cut off from Israel" (Ex. 12:15). Disobedience to the divine command carried severe consequences indeed. And again it was commanded, "Unleavened bread shall be eaten seven days. And no leavened bread shall be seen among you, nor shall leaven be seen among you *in all your quarters*" (Ex. 13:7). The extent of the restriction was further emphasized: "And no leaven shall be seen among you *in all your territory* for seven days" (Dt. 16:4).

The clarity of God's command allows no room for debate. Any leaven, no matter how small the amount or how discreet its presence, is not permitted during the Feast of Unleavened Bread. It is not enough to simply refrain from eating leaven, or from touching leaven, or even from looking at leaven by storing it away in a hidden place. All leaven must be purged out. Failure to do so is a serious breach of biblical law.

■ ■■■■ THE MODERN OBSERVANCE

Observant Jewish households begin their painstaking preparations weeks before the arrival of Passover. Walls are washed and painted, cooking utensils are scalded, clothing is washed with pockets turned inside out, carpets are cleaned, vacuum bags are discarded, and even special china dishes are brought out for the feast. Everything is scrubbed, scoured, cleaned, and aired in preparation.

On the night before Passover eve, after evening prayers in the synagogue, the father of each household will perform the *Bedikat Hametz*, or "Search for Leaven" ceremony. This ancient ceremony purges the last vestiges of leaven from the house. Earlier that evening, each mother will place a few bits of bread in several corners or on window sills of the house so that there will be some leaven present to be found.

After reciting the benediction for the occasion, the father begins the search. He uses an old wooden spoon in one hand and a goose feather in the other. By candlelight, he searches from room to room to discover the distributed bread scraps. The children follow behind with great excitement as he carefully uses the feather to sweep the bread he finds onto the wooden spoon. Finally, the bits of bread, the wooden spoon, and the feather are placed inside a bag or wrapped in a cloth. This is tied with a thread and set aside to be burned the next morning.

I vividly remember watching this ceremony one evening in Israel. I was living on the fourth floor of an apartment building not far from Montefiore's Windmill of the artists' quarter in Jerusalem. It was the night before Passover, and the day had been filled with the hustle and bustle of the approaching holiday. At dusk I heard the laughter of men and the voices of children through the back window of the apartment. As I looked from the balcony to the vacant lot below, the bright warm blaze of a bonfire caught my attention. A group of fathers were gathered around it with their children. As time went by, more men slowly drifted from surrounding apartment buildings to join the cheery circle. As each one tossed an armload of bread loaves onto the fire, the flames shot higher, sending a shower of streaking orange sparks into the cool April sky. The night wore on, and slowly the circle diminished in size as the men and children returned to their homes.

In the brightness of the morning sun, all that remained were the smoldering gray ashes of the fire and the sooty, charred remains of bread loaves — a stark reminder that in a few short hours Passover would begin. Soon, however, each of the men reappeared to toss a small bag of bread scraps into the ashes. A thin wisp of smoke turned to thick, billowing white smoke and then to tongues of fire, consuming the last of the leaven. With the biblical command fulfilled and all leaven purged from their homes, the way was clear for the arrival of Passover and the Feast of Unleavened Bread.

THE FULFILLMENT

Sin is often pictured as leaven in Scripture (Mt. 16:6,11; Mk. 8:15; Lk. 12:1; Gal. 5:9). The ancient rabbis also believed that "leaven represents the evil impulse of the heart" (Berachot 17a). Leaven is well-suited as a picture of sin since it rapidly permeates the dough, contaminating it, souring it, fermenting it, and swelling it to many times its original size without changing its weight. In fact, this souring process (the first stage of decay) is operative solely because of the curse of death decreed by God when Adam sinned.

Since leaven pictures sin, only *unleavened* bread (matzah) was used in the Temple (Lev. 2:11; 6:16-17; 10:12). Offerings had to be pure, and anything leavened was deemed impure and unfit.

As with the other feasts of the Lord in Leviticus 23, the prophetic meaning of the Feast of Unleavened Bread is found in the work of the Messiah. Passover pictures the substitutionary *death* of the Messiah as the Passover

Lamb, the Feast of Unleavened Bread pictures the *burial* of the Messiah, and Firstfruits pictures the *resurrection* of the Messiah.

The Hebrew prophets foretold a day when the Messiah would be a sacrifice for sin. He would be the Lamb offered up by God as the once-for-all sacrifice. The prophet declared of the Messiah: "Surely He has borne our griefs And carried our sorrows . . . the LORD has laid on Him the iniquity of us all . . . When You make His soul an offering for sin" (Isa. 53:4, 6, 10).

But the Hebrew prophets also spoke of Messiah's amazing burial. Isaiah prophesied, "And they made [appointed] His grave with the wicked – But [was instead] with the rich [one] at His death, Because he had done no violence [wickedness], Nor was any deceit in His mouth" (Isa. 53:9).

Normally, one who dies a criminal's death receives a criminal's burial.

But this was not the case with the Messiah. The Messiah was executed as if He were a criminal, but God did not allow His body to be cast outside the city onto the garbage heap. The Messiah was honored in His burial because He was a pure, sinless (without leaven) sacrifice. He died not for His own transgressions (He was innocent), but for ours (we are guilty). Therefore, God honored the Messiah with burial in a rich man's tomb. The Messiah was buried in the tomb of Joseph of Arimathaea (Mt. 27:57-60), a member of the Sanhedrin. This was God's statement upon the innocence of the Messiah.

But there is further significance surrounding the burial of the Messiah in that His body did not return to dust. King David prophesied of the Messiah: "For You will not leave my soul in [the grave], Nor will You allow Your Holy One [the Messiah] to see corruption [decay]" (Ps. 16:10). Obviously, King David did not prophesy this of himself. His grave has been a revered site in Jerusalem for almost 3,000 years. David's body did decay (as has the body of every other person who has died in history), but the Messiah's body did not. The sons of Adam are sinners under the divine curse: "To dust you shall return" (Gen. 3:19). As a pure, sinless sacrifice, the Messiah was not under the curse to return to dust. Therefore, the Messiah came forth from the grave on the third day after He had carried our sins far away (Ps. 103:12; Heb. 9:26).

The Messiah fulfilled the Feast of Unleavened Bread in that He was a pure, sinless (without leaven) sacrifice. God validated this by the Messiah's burial in a rich man's tomb. Furthermore, the body of the Messiah was not permitted to decay in the grave (like dough soured by leaven), but was brought forth because He was not a sinner under the curse of death and decay.

■ ■■■■■ THE APPLICATION

It is interesting that Paul used the purging ceremony for leaven to convey spiritual truth to the believers in the city of Corinth: "Therefore purge out the old leaven, that you may be a new lump, since you truly are unleavened. For indeed Christ, our Passover, was sacrificed for us. Therefore, let us keep the feast, not with old leaven, nor with the leaven of malice and wickedness, but with the unleavened bread of sincerity and truth" (1 Cor. 5:7-8).

Paul's message is simple and direct. For believers who have, by faith, accepted the sacrifice of the Passover Lamb upon Calvary, Passover is past history. The deliverance by Messiah, the true Passover Lamb, has already been experienced in their lives. They are now living in the Feast of

Unleavened Bread where purity and separation from leaven are required.

But Paul expresses shock and dismay that the Corinthian believers were still partaking of their old sins. It does no good to simply get rid of the large conspicuous loaves on the table and leave the little pieces of leaven scattered on the floor. A little leaven will contaminate everything else. "Do you not know that a little leaven leavens the whole lump?" (1 Cor. 5:6). He commands them to purge it out — all of it. In other words he pleads: "How can you enter into the Feast of Unleavened Bread still eating your leavened bread? It is not kosher. It does not belong. The two do not go together. It is an outrage! Get rid of it!"

Paul is simply stating what he later taught in Romans 6:1-18. The believer is no longer under the power (dominion) of sin — it has been broken. The believer is no longer a helpless slave to sin but rather chooses to sin when he is drawn away by his own lust (Jas. 1:14-15). The tragedy is that far too few believers realize this truth. They continue to be duped by the flesh into thinking and acting as if sin is still the evil taskmaster that they are obligated to obey.

In God's sight we are now unleavened (justified and pure) and are called to lives of holiness. So Paul questions, "Why keep living as if we are not?"

Again my mind goes back to Passover in Israel. It was the eighth day of the Passover season (the last day of the Feast of Unleavened Bread) and there was no "real" food in the house. My friend and I were tired of matzah, salads, and scrambled eggs. Since the grocery would not be selling bread until the following day, we caught a bus to downtown Jerusalem hoping to fare better. Imagine our disappointment when we discovered that our favorite pizza shop was still closed for Passover. Our hopes rose as we saw an open hamburger cafe, but they were dashed as we received our hamburgers on steamed matzah.

Not to be defeated, my friend suggested picking up a loaf of bread at the Arab market. So what would it hurt? Only a few hours, and it would be sundown anyway. He purchased two long loaves of bread, and they were placed in a cellophane shopping bag with the ends sticking out. On our way home, we cut through a grassy park to enjoy the scenery. As we passed a group of university students studying on the lawn, they became excited and began to shout at us in Hebrew. Innocently, we presumed that we were not allowed to walk on the grass and hurried on our way.

When we caught the bus it was crowded, and my friend and I were forced to sit in separate seats. Suddenly, I noticed that all the passengers were scowling at my friend and eyeing the bag of bread. This fact was obvious to my friend as well, for his face was flushed, and he was sunken down in his seat. Fortunately, the bus was not stopping at an ultraorthodox neighborhood, or our lives would surely have been endangered.

The presence of any leaven during Passover and the Feast of Unleavened Bread is an absolute outrage. Even the mere sight of it is a very serious matter.

So, a timely lesson on sin is found in Paul's admonition. Just as is done in the purging ceremony, we need to thoroughly sweep out our lives. It is not sufficient to simply throw out the conspicuous loaves on the table and hide the favorite loaf of rye in the cupboard or allow the unnoticed crumbs to remain under the stove. We need to take the candle of God's Word and search our lives. Every corner, every crack, and every window sill must be scrutinized in its light. The task is not complete until every speck of leaven is purged. Why? Paul gives the pressing motivation: "For indeed Christ, our Passover, was sacrificed for us" (1 Cor. 5:7).

בכורים

"Ye shall bring a sheaf of the first fruits of your harvest unto the priest, And he shall wave the sheaf before the LORD" (Lev. 23:10-11).

The Feast of Firstfruits

Kevin L. Howard

One division of systematic theology or major Bible doctrines is known as Eschatology, or literally, *the study of last things*. This vital area of biblical doctrine delves into future prophetic events in Scripture such as the Rapture of the Church, the Day of the Lord, the return of the Messiah, the restoration of Israel, and the messianic Kingdom. The entire study is devoted to *last things*.

Although not a major discipline, nor often examined, the subject of *first things* is one about which the Bible has much to say. Somewhat obscure and essentially unobserved for almost two thousand years, Israel's Feast of Firstfruits was an ancient holy day solely devoted to first things. Its powerful message and timeless truths provide a rich study for God's people today.

 ## THE BIBLICAL OBSERVANCE

The Meaning of Firstfruits

Firstfruits marked the beginning of the cereal grain harvests in Israel. Barley was the first grain to ripen of those sown in the winter months. For Firstfruits, a sheaf of barley was harvested and brought to the Temple as a thanksgiving offering to the Lord for the harvest. It was representative of the barley harvest as a whole and served as a pledge or guarantee that the remainder of the harvest would be realized in the days that followed.

The Time of Firstfruits

Firstfruits was an early spring feast, the third in the Jewish festive cycle. On the Hebrew calendar, it occurred on the 16th day of Nisan, the first biblical month (March or April), only two days after the beginning of the Passover season.

Scripture did not specify the actual calendar date of Firstfruits, but merely prescribed its time of observance to be "on the day after the Sabbath" (Lev. 23:11). This led to various interpretations and considerable debate as to which *sabbath* was in view.

The Sadducees, and later the Karaite Jews, understood it to refer to the first weekly sabbath (Saturday) which occurred during the week of Passover season. However, the word *sabbath* also designated any holy day on which work was prohibited, no matter on which day of the week it occurred (Lev. 23:24, 32, 39). The majority opinion, held by the Pharisees, was that the *sabbath* in question was Nisan 15, the first day of the Feast of Unleavened Bread. That day was to be "a holy convocation" (Lev. 23:7) on which no work was performed. This same description was given to the weekly sabbath (Lev. 23:3) and to holy-day sabbaths held on other days of the week (Lev. 23:24-25, 28, 32, 36, 39).

Ancient Jewish observance agreed with this interpretation. Josephus, the first-century Jewish historian, wrote: "But on the second day of unleavened bread, which is the sixteenth day of the month, they first partake of the fruits of the earth, for before that day they do not touch them" (*Antiquities of the Jews* 3.10.5).

Thus, the chronology of the Passover season consisted of: Passover (Nisan 14), the Feast of Unleavened Bread (7 days, Nisan 15-21), and the Feast of Firstfruits (Nisan 16). The second day of the Feast of Unleavened Bread (Nisan 16) was also Firstfruits, a day simultaneously shared by both holidays.

N I S A N

1	2	3	4	5	6	7
8	9	10	11	12	13	14 PASSOVER
15	16 FIRSTFRUITS	17	18	19	20	21
		FEAST OF UNLEAVENED BREAD				
22	23	24	25	26	27	28
29	30					

The Record of Firstfruits

The *regulations* for Firstfruits were outlined by the Lord in Leviticus 23:9-14. A sheaf (Heb. *omer*, meaning "measure") was to be brought to the priest at the Temple who would wave it before the Lord for acceptance. There were also to be accompanying sacrifices: an unblemished male lamb of the first year, a drink offering of wine, and a meal offering of the barley flour mixed with olive oil.

The people were forbidden to use any part of the harvest in any way until after the firstfruits were offered to the Lord (Lev. 23:14). To neglect these firstfruit offerings (or any others) was considered robbery of God according to Scripture (Mal. 3:8).

The *ritual* for the Firstfruits ceremony was detailed in Deuteronomy 26:1-10. The order of the worship ceremony, even the actual wording of the thanksgiving prayer to God, was carefully recorded in that text.

The Importance of Firstfruits

Firstfruits was preeminently seen as a time marker. It marked the beginning of the grain harvest in Israel, but even more importantly, it marked the countdown to the Feast of Weeks, the fourth of Israel's annual feasts. Beginning with Firstfruits, forty-nine days (or seven sevens) were counted, and on the fiftieth day, the Feast of Weeks was celebrated. The Lord commanded: "'And you shall count for yourselves from the day after the Sabbath, from the day that you brought the sheaf of the wave offering: seven Sabbaths shall be completed. Count fifty days to the day after the seventh Sabbath'" (Lev. 23:15-16).

As a result, this period of time was, and still is, known as the *Sefirat Ha-Omer* (Heb. "the Counting of the Omer") because of the ritual of counting the days from the *omer* (Heb. "sheaf, measure") to the Feast of Weeks.

The Service of Firstfruits

For the Nation

The Preparation for Firstfruits

In Temple days, Nisan 14 brought the painstaking preparations for the Passover season to completion:

lambs had been chosen for Passover sacrifices, houses had been purged of all leaven in preparation for the Feast of Unleavened Bread, and barley sheaves had been marked in the fields for the Feast of Firstfruits.

With each passing week, the weather in Israel turned noticeably warmer. Winter rains had ceased, and cloudy days had quickly become few and far between. Looking eastward from the Temple, one could see the breathtaking panorama of the Mount of Olives and the intervening Kidron Valley basking in the bright golden rays of the springtime sun. Across the Kidron in an area known as the Ashes Valley, a small, open field of amber barley nestled itself against a background of grassy, green slopes and misty gray olive trees. The ripe grain, swaying gently in the soft breeze, created a relaxing, mesmerizing pattern of warm gold. At one end of the field, several bundles of barley were conspicuously marked and tied together, still uncut, in anticipation of the coming Feast of Firstfruits.

This barley field was a special field, cultivated solely for the national Firstfruits offering and kept strictly in accordance with all rabbinic traditions. It had been plowed in the autumn and sown with barley some seventy days earlier during the winter months. Constant oversight assured that the crop had grown naturally, with no artificial watering or fertilization. In the days leading up to Passover, several sheaves were selectively marked and bundled by representatives from the Sanhedrin, Israel's ruling religious body. With that, the preparation for Firstfruits was complete.

The Procession of Firstfruits

$\mathcal{S}$everal days later at sundown on Nisan 15 (the beginning of the new Jewish day, Nisan 16), a three-man delegation from the Sanhedrin emerged from the Temple area, accompanied by a multitude of excited observers. The procession made its way down to the barley field to perform the Firstfruits reaping ceremony. With sickles in hand and baskets under arm, the three chosen reapers positioned themselves in readiness before the predetermined bundles of barley. As they did so, a hush fell over the crowd in recognition of the solemnity of the moment. Only the soft whisper of the swaying grain could be heard. Suddenly, the unison voices of the reapers broke the stillness of the evening with a series of questions to the onlookers: "Has the sun set?" "With this sickle?" "Into this basket?" "On this Sabbath?" "Shall I reap (now)?" Having received affirmative responses, the priests repeated this final verification process twice again as a safeguard. The marked sheaves were then reaped until one ephah of barley (approximately $^2/_3$ bushel) was obtained.

The Presentation of Firstfruits

In the Temple court, the grain was threshed with rods rather than oxen-drawn sledges so that the barley corns would not be injured. It was then parched over an open flame and winnowed in the wind to remove the chaff. Finally, the barley was milled and put through an intensive sifting process until sifted very fine. According to the Talmud, this sifting ceremony continued until one of the Temple inspectors could plunge his hands into the flour and remove them without any flour adhering to his hands (Menahot 8:2).

On the morning of Nisan 16, the firstfruits were presented to the Lord. One omer (about five pints) of the barley flour was mixed with $^3/_4$ pint of olive oil, and a small amount of frankincense was sprinkled upon it. This became the Firstfruits offering. The priest waved it before the Lord in accordance with Leviticus 23:11-13 and burned a small amount upon the altar. The remainder was given to the Levites.

For the Family

Firstfruits was a national observance, but each family brought its respective Firstfruits offering to the Temple as well. Early each spring, Israelite farmers performed the ritual of setting their firstfruits apart. Throughout the terraced hill country of Ephraim and Judah, and rolling hills of the lowlands, the ritual was frequently repeated. Farmers, followed by skipping children, ventured into the fields to mark the best of their unripened crops. A rush or cord was carefully tied around the selected firstfruits so as not to damage them. These were set apart to the Lord as each farmer declared, "Behold, these are the firstfruits." Excitement mounted daily as the firstfruits ripened and were finally harvested for the Passover pilgrimage to Jerusalem.

On the morning of Nisan 16, the winding streets of Jerusalem were alive with the smell of baking *matzah*, the sound of laughing children, the excited shouts of a woman, a baby's cry, the distant barking of a dog, the nervous bleating of sheep, and the soft cooing of turtledoves. Jerusalem was waking to the Feast of Firstfruits.

The early spring morning was cool, the air still calm. A slight haze hung in the air, slowly dissipating in the brightness of the morning sun. The towering Temple, with its radiant white marble columns and golden brass trim, was situated like a glistening diadem on the brow of Mount

Zion. Outside its gates, the haunting melody of flutes quickened the hearts of those who arrived, evoking the traditional joyful reply: "Praise God in His sanctuary" (Ps. 150:1). Inside the Temple gates, Levitical choirs led the worship music with Psalm 30: "I will extol You, O LORD, for You have lifted me up, And have not let my foes rejoice over me. . . ." That scene would continue throughout the day as the Jewish nation flocked to the sanctuary of the Lord.

Glancing into the Court of the Priests **c**, one could see orange flames on the sacrificial altar **e** leaping toward heaven as a column of steam and blue smoke drifted slowly toward the east. A host of priests were present there: some tending the fires, some slaughtering the sacrifices, some pouring the drink offerings, and some waving the Firstfruits offerings before the Lord.

In the Court of the Israelites **d**, a steady stream of men could be seen on the fifteen steps of the Nicanor Gate **f**, solemnly presenting their offerings to the priests under its impressive archway. Many led small white lambs on ropes. Some of the men were obviously poor, as was conspicuous by their simple clothing. One such man, Yehuda ben Sabba, a young, rugged farmer, stepped forward and said with great feeling: "Let everything that has breath praise the LORD." As he did so, he handed a rough wooden cage to an attending priest. Two turtledoves were tied inside as the alternate burnt offering for those too poor to afford a lamb (Lev. 5:7; 12:8; 14:22). As the priest held the turtledoves, the young farmer accompanied his offering with a prayer to God, confessing his sin.

Yehuda intently watched the preparation of his sacrifice in accordance with the Law of Moses (Lev. 1:14-17). Each step was completed accurately, quickly, and with obvious familiarity on the part of the priest. Yehuda watched the priest carefully drain the blood at the side of the altar. He saw the plucked crop feathers drift to the ground and rest on the pile of ashes beside the altar, awaiting removal to a place outside the city. Finally, with one smooth motion, he observed the priest cleave each bird down the breastbone and lay it upon the sacrificial fire.

As he gazed at the resulting puff of white steam, Yehuda's mind drifted back over the centuries to his father Abraham. He wondered if perhaps his burnt offering now lay on the exact spot where God had graciously provided the ram as a substitute for Isaac.

The movement of the returning priest caught his attention and interrupted the momentary daydream. Standing face-to-face with the priest, Yehuda repeated the familiar Firstfruits prayer. In a clear, Hebrew tongue he proclaimed: "'I declare today to the LORD your God that I have come to the country which the LORD swore to our fathers to give us'" (Dt. 26:3).

Then Yehuda removed the basket from his shoulder and handed it to the priest. The simple basket of peeled willow shoots contained the omer of barley for his Firstfruits offering. The priest placed his hands under the basket and slowly waved it before the Lord as Yehuda continued his ceremonial prayer: "'My father was a Syrian, about to perish, and he went down to Egypt and dwelt there, few in number; and there he became a nation, great, mighty, and populous. He has brought us to this place and has given us this land, "a land flowing with milk and honey"; and now, behold, I have brought the firstfruits of the land which you, O LORD, have given me'" (Dt. 26:5,9-10).

With the thanksgiving prayer complete, the priest set the basket in front of the altar and cast a handful of the grain upon the fire. Yehuda fell on his face to worship the Lord, then returned to the outer courts to rejoin his family. Seeing their father, his children ran and clutched his knees. The commandments for the holy day were now fulfilled. Yehuda and his excited family departed, rejoicing in the new harvest from the Lord. And so the experience went for hundreds of thousands throughout that ancient day of Firstfruits.

THE MODERN OBSERVANCE

Firstfruits sacrifices and offerings are not offered today since there is no Temple. The only Firstfruits ritual which has survived to modern times has been the counting of the omer, the days from Firstfruits to Shavuot (the Feast of Weeks).

On the thirty-third day of this period, a minor holiday called *Lag B'Omer* is celebrated. The first word of this holiday is a combination of the Hebrew letters *lamed* and *gimmel* (which numerically represent thirty-three) since the holiday occurs on the thirty-third day.

The origins of this joyous holiday are very obscure. The Talmud suggests that it was on this day that a plague ended among the students of the second-century rabbi, Akiba. To remember that happy day, Lag B'Omer is a favorite day on which to perform weddings. It is also customary in Israel to build campfires at night and stay up singing songs and roasting potatoes over the campfire. Israeli building contractors cringe at the approach of this holiday, for usually every scrap of unguarded wood on their job sites is scavenged by neighborhood children for firewood.

Jewish mystics also commemorate this day as the anniversary of the death of Rabbi Simeon bar Yochai, the author of their book on mysticism. Many thousands traditionally visit the rabbi's grave site in Meron (in northern

Israel) on Lag B'Omer. This is especially true among the Satmar, a particular sect of ultraorthodox Jews. Multitudes of the Satmar fly to Israel from Brooklyn each Lag B'Omer to visit the rabbi's grave.

I remember one Lag B'Omer season, sitting in the Paris airport waiting for the next flight to Israel. There were scores of Satmar milling about,

having just completed their morning prayer service. As I sat there, I met a young man and began to inquire about his plans in Israel. As we were talking, a young child with shoulder-length blond hair ran up to my Satmar friend. I remember being somewhat intrigued by the blond hair, a not-too-common sight among Jewish children. I asked the man if this was his daughter. He replied, "No, this is my *nephew*." My friend saw the momentary puzzlement on my face. He reminded me that it is customary among Jewish mystics for three-year-old boys to receive their first haircut on Lag B'Omer while at the rabbi's grave. This is to somehow bring them good luck.

Apart from the counting of the days, there is no modern celebration of Firstfruits.

■ ▇▇▇▇ THE APPLICATION

First Things in General

First things are an important and oft-repeated theme of Scripture. God declared that, in general, the firstfruits of all agricultural produce belonged to Him, from grain, to wine, to oil, to fleece (Ex. 22:29; 23:19; 34:26; Dt. 18:4; 26:2). This included all of the seven major crops of the land of Israel: barley, wheat, grapes, figs, pomegranates, olives, and dates. The firstfruits of the bread dough also belonged to Him as "a heave offering" (Num. 15:20-21). Further still, the firstborn males of all animals (Ex. 22:30; Lev. 27:26) and, indeed, even the firstborn of the Israelites themselves, belonged to Him (Ex. 13:2, 12-15; 34:19-20; Num. 3:13; 18:15-16).

According to the Mosaic Law, each firstborn male was to be presented to the priest at one month of age (Num. 18:16). In His mercy, the Lord made provision so that the firstborn could be redeemed and thus freed from lifetime service to God. At this dedication ceremony, called a *Pidyon Haben* (Heb. "Redemption of the Son"), it was possible to redeem the son out of full-time service through the payment of five shekels (pieces of silver) to the priest (Num. 18:16). The Pidyon Haben held true for all except priests and Levites. They were obligated to serve in the Temple and, therefore, could not be exempted.

At one month of age, Jesus was taken to the Temple for His Pidyon Haben. Mary and Joseph presented Him to the Lord: "As it is written in the law of the Lord, 'Every male who opens the womb shall be called holy to the LORD'" (Lk. 2:23).

Significantly, it was on this occasion that Jesus was first publicly declared to be the Messiah. The godly Simeon took the Child in his arms and blessed God: "For my eyes have seen Your salvation" (Lk. 2:30). As a second witness, Anna, the prophetess, declared His messiahship "to all those who looked for redemption in Jerusalem" (Lk. 2:38).

The meaning of the Pidyon Haben ceremony was given by the Lord: "Because all the firstborn are Mine. On the day that I struck all the firstborn in the land of Egypt, I sanctified to Myself all the firstborn in Israel" (Num. 3:13).

When God redeemed Israel out of Egyptian bondage, He did so through the blood of the Passover lamb. All firstborn were under the curse of death and judgment. Escape was possible only by exhibiting faith in God through the blood of the innocent Passover lamb (Ex. 12:12-13).

So, too, in the spiritual sense, all men are firstborn. All are sinners just as Adam and, therefore, are under the curse of death and in need of redemption (Rom. 5:17, 19; 1 Cor. 15:22). Escape is possible only by exhibiting faith in God through the redemptive blood of the Messiah, the true Passover Lamb, sacrificed as our substitute (1 Cor. 5:7).

Firstfruits in the New Testament

Although not as strongly emphasized in the Hebrew Scriptures as the other Levitical feasts, the Feast of Firstfruits forms an important backdrop to New Testament teaching. It is directly mentioned on no less than seven occasions in the New Testament.

Paul spoke of Epaenetus as "the firstfruits of Achaia" (Rom. 16:5). That is, Epaenetus was the first of many to trust in Jesus in western Asia Minor. Paul later spoke of the household of Stephanas as the "firstfruits of Achaia" (1 Cor. 16:15). They were also some of the first believers in that large and bountiful harvest in Asia Minor.

Elsewhere, Paul used the concept of the firstfruits pinched from the dough to teach: "For if the firstfruit is holy, the lump is also holy" (Rom. 11:16). By this he meant, if God chose and accepted the patriarchs, then the whole lump of dough (Israel) belonged to Him. Therefore, "God has not cast away His people" (Rom. 11:2).

Speaking of believers as *set apart* to the Lord, James taught: "Of His own will He brought us forth by the word of truth, that we might be a kind of firstfruits of His creatures" (Jas. 1:18).

Paul again used this imagery when he spoke of salvation as the "first-fruits of the Spirit" (Rom. 8:23). By this he meant that the indwelling of the Spirit of God is the guarantee, or pledge, that there will be a final redemption. Our bodies will be glorified and the creation redeemed from the curse. The present reality of the indwelling of believers by the Holy Spirit assures, or guarantees (is the firstfruits of), the future promise of Heaven.

In the Book of Revelation, John described a special group of 144,000 Jewish men who will be sealed just prior to the opening of the seventh seal (Rev. 7:1-8). There will be 12,000 from each of the various tribes of Israel, sealed and protected from God's wrath at the commencement of the Day of the Lord. Later, John describes these 144,000 as "the ones who follow the Lamb wherever He goes. These were redeemed from among men, being firstfruits to God and to the Lamb" (Rev. 14:4).

But how are these 144,000 considered firstfruits? Immediately after the

Rapture of the Church, the 144,000 will be God's first working with national Israel. They will be the proof, guarantee, or pledge (the firstfruits) of a future harvest within the nation of Israel. They will be the guarantee during the time of God's awesome wrath that He has not cast off His people. God will burn away the chaff and impurities in the fiery blast furnace of His wrath to bring the remnant of Israel to repentance at the end of Daniel's seventieth week. Paul summarizes the result: "And so all Israel will be saved" (Rom. 11:26).

Identifying with Israel's final harvest, Paul spoke of himself as "one born out of due time" (1 Cor. 15:8). The imagery was that of a fig tree which would occasionally yield prematurely ripened figs out of season. These early figs were few and rare. Paul viewed himself as one of these whom God had graciously saved before the final harvest.

■ ▨▨▨ THE FULFILLMENT

Like Israel's other spring feasts, the Feast of Firstfruits found its prophetic fulfillment in the work of Messiah's first coming. Paul declared this in the seventh and *most significant* reference to firstfruits in the New Testament with his glorious proclamation, "But now Christ is risen from the dead, and has become the firstfruits of those who have fallen asleep" (1 Cor. 15:20; cf. Rev. 1:5).

But how was the Messiah our firstfruits? Jesus rose again on the third day (literally, the third day of Passover season, Nisan 16), on the day of the Firstfruits. But His resurrection had far greater implications. Paul explained, "For as in Adam all die, even so in Christ all shall be made alive" (1 Cor. 15:22). The resurrection of Jesus is the guarantee and the beginning (firstfruits) of the final harvest, or resurrection, of all mankind. The Messiah fulfilled the prophetic meaning of this holy day by rising from the dead to become the firstfruits of the resurrection, and He did it on the very day of Firstfruits.

The Bible clearly teaches that there is life after death. The human spirit does not cease to exist, nor does it float aimlessly as part of some "cosmic consciousness," nor is it even reincarnated. All will be resurrected. Only the quality of that eternal existence remains in question. The Hebrew prophet, Daniel, prophesied: "And many of those who sleep in the dust of the earth shall awake, Some to everlasting life, Some to shame and everlasting contempt" (Dan. 12:2).

The Messiah further explained: "Do not marvel at this; for the hour is coming in which all who are in the graves will hear His voice and come forth — those who have done good, to the resurrection of life, and those who have done evil, to the resurrection of condemnation" (Jn. 5:28-29).

Just as there are two parts to the harvest, the wheat and the chaff, there will be two parts to the final harvest (Mt. 3:12; 13:37-43). Some will inherit eternal life and dwell in the house of the Lord forever. Others will inherit eternal separation from God, confined forever to the Lake of Fire. They that belong to the Messiah, who have by faith trusted in Him, will be resurrected unto life at His coming (1 Cor. 15:23; cf. Isa 25:8; 1 Th. 4:16). Jesus provided the ironclad guarantee when He rose from the dead. It will happen, of that we are sure, because "now is Christ risen from the dead, and has become the firstfruits of those who have fallen asleep."

שבועות

"And you shall observe the Feast of Weeks,
of the firstfruits of wheat harvest" (Ex. 34:22).

Shavuot – The Feast of Weeks

Kevin L. Howard

Holidays are almost universally celebrated on specific calendar dates. For example, New Year's Day is always January 1, and America's Independence Day is always July 4. Likewise, one does not usually count the number of days between holidays. However, just the opposite is true for the Jewish feast of Shavuot, Israel's fourth holy day. No date is associated with it in the Bible. Yet, ask any observant Jew concerning Shavuot and he will answer that it is always celebrated fifty days after the Feast of Firstfruits.

THE BIBLICAL OBSERVANCE

The Meaning of Shavuot

Names were very important in the ancient Jewish world. They usually reflected the significant character, history, or meaning of that to which they were attached. Three separate names were used by the Hebrew Scriptures for the feast of *Shavuot* (Heb. "weeks"). Each name emphasized a different facet of its observance.

The most common Hebrew designation was *Hag Hashavuot*, meaning "the Feast of Weeks" (Ex. 34:22; Dt. 16:10; 2 Chr. 8:13). Shavuot was called the Feast of Weeks because seven *weeks* were counted from the Feast of Firstfruits until observing this feast.

The primary meaning of the feast was reflected in the Hebrew name, *Yom Habikkurim* or "the Day of Firstfruits" (Num. 28:26), since Shavuot was the day on which the firstfruit offerings of the summer wheat crop were brought to the Temple. Thus, Shavuot marked the beginning of the summer wheat harvest even as Israel's earlier Feast of Firstfruits marked the beginning of the spring barley harvest.

The third designation, *Hag Hakatzir* or "the Feast of Harvest" (Ex.

23:16), reflected the fact that this festival was the official beginning of the summer harvest season.

In addition to the biblical designations, the Talmud and Josephus referred to this festival as *Atzeret*, meaning "conclusion." They viewed Shavuot as the conclusion of the Passover season and of the seven-week spring harvest since there are no other major Jewish holy days until the autumn.

In the Greek language, Shavuot was known as *Pentecost* (Acts 2:1; 2 Macc. 12:32), meaning "fiftieth," since it was celebrated on the fiftieth day from the Feast of Firstfruits.

The Time of Shavuot

Shavuot is observed in the late spring, usually late May or early June. On the modern Hebrew calendar, Shavuot falls on the sixth day of the month of Sivan. As noted earlier, the celebration of Shavuot was never tied to an actual calendar date in the Bible. It was instead defined as a calculation of fifty days (the day after seven weeks had passed) from the Feast of Firstfruits: "'And you shall count . . . fifty days to the day after the seventh Sabbath'" (Lev. 23:15-16; cf. Dt. 16:9-10).

Because of the commandment to count, the time period from Firstfruits to Shavuot is known as *Sefirah* (Heb. "counting"). The measure of barley which was brought to the Temple as a firstfruit offering on the Feast of Firstfruits was known as the *omer* (Heb. "measure, sheaf"). Since this counting of days was to begin with the offering of the omer, this fifty-day period is also known as "the omer."

The Record of Shavuot

Three Scripture passages outline the biblical observance for Shavuot. Temple offerings were described in Leviticus 23:15-21 and Numbers 28:26-31. The requirements for individual worshipers were outlined in Deuteronomy 16:9-12 where they were instructed to offer a freewill offering, to rejoice before the Lord, and to remember that the Lord had freed them from Egyptian bondage.

The Importance of Shavuot

In Bible days, Shavuot was a particularly important Jewish feast. Seven divinely appointed feasts were given to Israel. Of these seven, three were decreed by the Lord as "solemn feasts" (Ex. 23:14-17; Dt. 16:16; 2 Chr. 8:13; cf. Ex. 34:22-23) during which all Israelite men were obligated to present themselves at the Temple. Shavuot was the second in this exclusive triad of solemn feasts, the others being Unleavened Bread and Tabernacles.

Like the Sabbath and many of the other feast days, Shavuot was a holy *convocation* or rest day (Lev. 23:21; Num. 28:26). Therefore, no work was permitted.

The Service of Shavuot

According to the Bible, it was forbidden to eat of the new barley crop until the barley firstfruits (omer) were offered on the Feast of Firstfruits. The same principle was applied to the wheat crop. Therefore, the numerous meal offerings and showbread for the sanctuary were not made from the new wheat crop until after the wheat firstfruits were presented on Shavuot.

The Temple services for Shavuot followed much the same pattern as that of the Feast of Firstfruits since both holy days were celebrated with firstfruit offerings. However, the offering for Shavuot was unique. It consisted of two long, flat, leavened loaves of wheat bread as commanded by the Lord: "'You shall bring from your dwellings two wave loaves of two-tenths of an ephah. They shall be of fine flour; they shall be baked with leaven. They are the firstfruits to the LORD'" (Lev. 23:17).

The loaves were not burned because the Lord had forbidden leaven on the altar: "'You shall burn no leaven nor any honey in any offering to the LORD made by fire'" (Lev. 2:11). Instead, these loaves and two lambs as a peace offering formed the wave offering for Shavuot. The priest waved them before the altar forwards and backwards, then up and down. Afterward, they were set aside "for the priest" (Lev. 23:20) and formed the festive meal eaten by the priests later that day in the Temple.

▧ ▬▬▬ THE MODERN OBSERVANCE

As with Israel's other holy days, customs and traditions were added over time. To understand these changes to Shavuot, a brief review of Jewish history is necessary.

Roman rule was never welcome in ancient Judea. It was despised and was an ever-increasing stench in the nose of the Jewish nation. And although a Jewish resistance movement was active for almost a century, it never seriously challenged the Roman eagle's grip until the year A.D. 66. During the summer heat of that year, the rebellion gained critical mass. Jerusalem was cleansed of Roman rule, and for three years a limited Jewish independence was restored.

The shock waves were felt throughout the mighty Roman Empire. Determined to make tiny Judea an object lesson to any other would-be rebel provinces, the Roman general Titus was dispatched to quell the uprising.

After a successful Roman siege, Jerusalem was viciously sacked, the Temple leveled, and the Jews were pushed out of their capital in A.D. 70. To ensure Roman control of Judea, a Roman garrison was permanently established on the ruins of Jerusalem.

The tremendous importance that the Romans attached to the fall of Jerusalem in A.D. 70 can be seen in their extensive media efforts. To proclaim this victory throughout the empire, thousands of coins were minted with the inscription "Judaea Capta." These coins depicted Judea as a woman weeping under a palm tree with a fettered Jewish captive standing to the side. It was common for Rome to issue victory coins, but many more were issued for this occasion than for its other conquests. In the city of Rome, the victory was commemorated by the construction of the massive Arch of Titus near the entrance to the Roman Forum. The elaborate relief sculptures over the top of the arch showed a great military parade of triumphant Roman soldiers carrying away the Temple treasures and Jewish captives to Rome. (The picture of

Roman soldiers holding up the golden menorah led the Israeli government in January 1996 to formally petition the Vatican to support an investigation of the holy lampstand's whereabouts as a symbol of reconciliation between the Jewish people and the Catholic church.) In any case, ancient Rome made certain that the example of Judah was prominently kept before the eyes of every citizen.

As the intervening years unfolded, the hot coals of Jewish nationalism continued to smolder below the surface. Tensions from the resulting harsh Roman rule finally appeared to ease when Hadrian became emperor in A.D. 117. Hadrian promised to restore Jerusalem and the holy Temple. The Jewish people hoped that they might at last recover from the terrible destruction of A.D. 70, but those hopes would soon go up in smoke.

Hadrian came under the influence of Greek culture (Hellenism) and became more and more anti-Semitic. As he did, his cruel repression of the Jewish people followed in the footsteps of Antiochus Epiphanes of almost 300 years earlier (see Hanukkah, Chapter 12). Hadrian outlawed circumcision, Sabbath observance, and synagogue prayers in an attempt to erase Jewish distinctives and assimilate the sons of Israel into the Roman empire.

In A.D. 130, Hadrian abandoned his promise. Jerusalem would be rebuilt, but only as a Roman city named after his chief deities. A house of worship would be built on the Temple Mount, but it would be a pagan shrine, patterned after the temple to Jupiter located in Rome.

There seemed to be only one alternative to the desperate situation. With the very existence of the Jewish people at stake, the second Jewish revolt against Rome was ignited. Jewish forces liberated Jerusalem in A.D. 132 under the brilliant leadership of Simon Bar Kochba.

Yet, despite his success, controversy surrounded Bar Kochba. Rabbi Akiba, the foremost rabbi of the day and the head of the Sanhedrin, declared Bar Kochba the Messiah. This set off a firestorm of debate among the rabbis and forced Jewish believers in Jesus to leave his ranks.

It is not mere coincidence that the Jewish coins minted during the Bar Kochba revolt bore the picture of the rebuilt Temple (the crown jewel of Israel's religion) and the inscription: "For the liberation of Jerusalem." Messianic fervor gripped much of the nation. Many believed that Israel's Golden Age was about to begin and that Bar Kochba would be the one to throw off Roman rule, rebuild the Temple, and lead the nation into the messianic Kingdom.

But such was not to be the case. In A.D. 133, the

Roman Legion counterattacked with its best force of 35,000 foot soldiers. For three years, the Roman army steadily squeezed the life from the zealot resistance movement. Finally, in A.D. 135, the uprising was suppressed. Bar Kochba made his last stand and was killed at his stronghold of Betar. As an act of savage brutality, Roman forces desecrated the thousands of dead by forbidding their burial.

When the smoke cleared, the legacy of devastation left behind was mind-numbing. It was beyond comprehension. Some 50 fortresses and 985 villages lay in ruins. The death toll in Jewish life from the war topped 580,000. Countless other lives were claimed by starvation and disease. Tens of thousands were sold into slavery. Jews were forbidden to enter their capital city under pain of death. Finally, Jerusalem was rebuilt as the heathen Aelia Capitolina. "Aelia" reflected the second name of Hadrian (Publius Aelius Hadrianus), indicating the city's dedication to imperial worship. "Capitolina" was a reminder that the city was also dedicated to the worship of the Roman gods of the Capitoline Hill (Jupiter, Minerva, and Juno). At the very heart of the paganized city, a temple to Jupiter (Satan) was erected on Mount Zion, desecrating the site of the holy Temple. In commemoration, Hadrian issued a Roman victory coin showing a yoke of oxen plowing the new foundations.

The momentary flickering candle of Jewish optimism was snuffed out by the iron fist of Rome. National hopes for independence and the rebuilding of the Temple were dashed. The nation was defeated, her people were dispersed, her homeland devastated. The land was desolate with nothing to harvest, but far more tragic, there was no Temple to which to bring the offerings. Without the Temple, the continued observance of Israel's feasts as outlined in the Law of Moses was impossible. As the gravity of the situation settled into the national consciousness, despair reigned.

Giving of Torah

Responding to this dire crisis, the Sanhedrin convened in A.D. 140 in the village of Usha near the modern city of Haifa. They decided to divert the focus of Shavuot observance away from agriculture and instead associate it with a historical event to keep the holiday alive. The rabbis suggested that Shavuot was the day that the Torah (Mosaic Law) was given to Moses on Mt. Sinai. This was not done arbitrarily. Although the Bible never associated Shavuot with Sinai, this theme was chosen because the giving of the Law had also occurred in the third month (Ex. 19:1).

Thus, the idea of the giving of the Law and the birthday of Judaism quickly caught on (as evidenced in ancient Jewish literature Shabbat 86b and Jubilees 6:19) and became the dominant motif of the modern Shavuot. And so Shavuot became known as *Zeman Mattan Toratenu*, "the Time of the Giving of Our Law."

Synagogue

It is customary to decorate synagogues with greenery and beautiful floral arrangements for Shavuot. Some synagogues hang an embroidered green curtain over the ark (where the scrolls are stored). Some synagogues braid a crown of branches and flowers for the Torah scrolls. Others weave a canopy of flowers over the reading area. The reason for these decorations is Shavuot's emphasis as a harvest festival. According to tradition, these are also a reminder that Mt. Sinai was at one time covered with green trees and grass.

The ancient Scripture readings for Shavuot (Ezek. 1:1-28; 3:12; Hab. 2:20-3:19) date back to the days of the Temple. They describe the brightness of God's glory. In Ezekiel's vision he witnessed wind, fire, and voices:

"Then I looked, and behold, a whirlwind was coming out of the north, a great cloud with raging fire engulfing itself; and brightness was all around it and radiating out of its midst like the color of amber, out of the midst of the fire . . . Then the Spirit lifted me up, and I heard behind me a great thunderous voice: 'Blessed is the glory of the LORD from His place!'" (Ezek. 1:4; 3:12).

Habakkuk saw the Lord revealed at the Messiah's coming in fire and bright light: "God came from Teman, The Holy One from Mount Paran . . . His glory covered the heavens . . . His brightness was like the light . . . And fever followed at His feet" (Hab. 3:3-5).

After Shavuot was refocused to the giving of the Law, Exodus 19-20 was included in the Shavuot Scripture readings. These chapters describe God's revelation on Mt. Sinai and the Ten Commandments. When the Ten Commandments are read in the synagogue service, it is customary to stand.

It is also a Shavuot custom to read the Book of Ruth in the synagogue. Several reasons are usually given. Most prominently, the story of Ruth took place during the spring barley harvest, and Shavuot is the celebration of the conclusion of the barley harvest and the beginning of the summer wheat harvest. Secondly, Ruth the Moabitess willingly embraced the God of Israel and His Law (the Torah). Therefore, her story is read on this holiday which today focuses on the giving of the Law. In this regard, many synagogues also hold Shavuot confirmation services for their teenage youth to recognize their childhood studies and confirm their commitment to live according to the Mosaic Law.

Food

One of the most popular Shavuot traditions is the eating of dairy foods. The rabbis have suggested that this widespread practice is a reminder of the Law, since the words of Scripture are like milk and honey to the soul.

Among the most delicious and tempting of these dairy dishes are cheesecakes, cheese blintzes, and cheese *kreplach*. The blintzes are made of cheese rolled in pancakes and fried in a skillet. The kreplach are dough pockets which are stuffed with cheese for Shavuot. These kreplach are similar to ravioli noodles, only triangular in shape. The three corners of the dumpling are said to recall the statement of the ancient rabbis: "Blessed be the Merciful One who gave the threefold law [Law, Prophets, and Writings] to a people made of three classes [priests, Levites, and Israelites], through a third-born child [Moses was born after Miriam and Aaron] in the third month [Sivan]" (Shabbat 88a).

It is also customary to bake two loaves of *hallah* bread on Shavuot. These represent the two loaves of bread offered in the Temple and the two tablets of the Law received on Mt. Sinai. A seven-rung ladder design is traditionally formed on the top of the loaves symbolizing the ascent of Moses to receive the Ten Commandments.

Stay up all night

It is customary today for observant Jews to stay up the entire night of Shavuot studying and discussing Torah. Traditionally, they study the opening and closing verses of each Sabbath reading, the opening and closing verses of each book of the Bible, and the entire Book of Ruth. Throughout the night there are periodic breaks for coffee and cheesecake.

As dawn approaches in Israel, thousands of observant Jews can be seen winding their way from the orthodox quarters of Jerusalem toward the site of the ancient Temple. These multitudes pour onto the Western Wall plaza to recite the ancient *Amidah* prayer together. The Amidah or "standing" prayer with its nineteen blessings dates back more than 2,000 years. It forms the central prayer of all prayer services (morning, afternoon, evening, Sabbath, and holidays).

THE FULFILLMENT

The year was around A.D. 30. It was a hot morning late in the month of May when the day of Shavuot came that year. The fiery topaz of a Judean sun was already high above the horizon, several hours along on its daily trek. A thin blanket of low-lying morning clouds had long since disappeared in the presence of its heat, leaving only a clear blue sky above Jerusalem.

In the stillness of the mid-morning air, the Temple *Shakharit* (morning) service could be heard as it concluded — the blast of silver trumpets, the thunder of worshipers praying in unison, the solitary voice of the reader chanting from Ezekiel and Habakkuk.

Throngs of Jewish worshipers crowded the Temple courts. Since Shavuot was a pilgrim holiday, many were conspicuously visiting from other countries throughout the Middle East, Northern Africa, Europe, and Asia.

Suddenly, from high overhead, the roar of a violent windstorm was heard. But how could this be? There were no clouds and there was no breeze. It was the wrong time of the year for a storm. The worshipers stood confused, searching the cloudless sky to find the source of the disturbance.

The sound began to change as if it were descending toward the west. Several hundred men in the outer court rushed out the southwest gate, past the Temple guards, and onto the towering steps leading down to the city below. From that lofty vantage point, the momentary flashes of what seemed like swirling bits of fire from one of the nearby houses below caught their attention. The men paused while shouting and pointing toward the house. What could this wind and fire mean? Could this be what they had just heard read from Ezekiel and Habakkuk? Could it be that the Shekinah glory was returning to Israel after some 600 years?

The crowd pushed onward, determined to know the matter. In a few moments they had reached the house and were pounding on the door. Had not twelve men from inside pushed their way to the street, the door surely would have been broken down.

The twelve immediately began to address a barrage of excited queries from the crowd. But to the astonishment of the crowd, the twelve answered in the various native languages of those within the crowd. This caused an uproar of discussion. These twelve were obviously Galilean by their style of dress, but who had ever heard of an educated Galilean? Education was centered in Jerusalem, not Capernaum. How were these uneducated Galileans able to speak not only the languages, but to speak them with the very accents as if they were their mother tongue? Many pressed for answers while others began to mock and accuse the men of drunkenness.

Word of the wind and fire had spread quickly to the teeming crowds who were now leaving the Temple service. The streets were filling fast, and communication was becoming impossible.

One of the twelve named Peter, apparently the spokesman, shouted for the crowd to follow him to the nearby plaza outside the southern entrance to the Temple. The site was a favorite place for the rabbis to teach their students before entering the Temple complex. With its surrounding plaza and low, 200-foot-wide steps leading up to the southern gate, the location was one of the best in the Temple area for addressing large crowds.

The twelve ascended to the landing of the white limestone steps, their backs to the magnificent three-tiered Royal Portico which towered 120 feet above them. By the time Peter lifted his hands to quiet the crowd, a sea of humanity was assembled on the plaza below. The locals recognized these Galileans as followers of Jesus of Nazareth, the One who had been crucified almost two months earlier at Passover.

The crowd fell silent and fixed their gaze upon Peter as he began to speak. "Men of Judea and all who live in Jerusalem, let me explain this to you; listen carefully to what I say. These men are not drunk, as you suppose. It's only nine in the morning! No, this is what was spoken by the prophet Joel: 'And it shall come to pass in the last days, says God, That I will pour out of My Spirit on all flesh; Your sons and your daughters shall prophesy.'"

He was right. They themselves had witnessed the signs of wind and fire and heard these twelve miraculously sharing the Scriptures in their own native dialects. Surely this was the hand of God.

Peter went on to quote the Hebrew prophet concerning the coming day of God's wrath and warn that only those who "call upon the name of the Lord shall be saved." This crowd of devoutly religious men remained silent. Only the distant bleating of sheep from somewhere in the Temple could be heard. There seemed to be an electricity in the air, an anticipation, even a hunger by the crowd for Peter to continue his words.

Peter turned his words toward Jesus of Nazareth, and for the next quarter hour he slowly, forcefully, and with a simple eloquence reasoned from the prophecies of King David and Israel's prophets concerning the promised Messiah. As he shared prophecy after prophecy, it became obvious that the Scriptures had clearly and convincingly foretold Messiah's death, resurrection, and ascension into Heaven. How could one believe otherwise?

The crowd of orthodox men was visibly moved and beginning to mill about. Peter's words burned within their hearts. Some had tears streaming down their cheeks. Some were slowly striking their chests with clenched hand as a sign of anguish and repentance. Others could bear it no longer and began to shout, "What should we do?" With strong emotion in his voice, Peter urged them, "Repent!" Motioning southward toward the nearby Pool of Siloam, he continued, "Then be immersed in the name of Jesus the Messiah because your sins are forgiven, and you will receive the Holy Spirit . . . for the promise is for you and your children."

Throughout the morning, scattered crowds could be seen in the plaza questioning and discussing with some of the twelve. Yet, what was truly overwhelming was to see the throngs of men streaming to and from the *mikvehs* (baptismal pools). In all, some 3,000 trusted in the Lord that morning.

The above is based on a true eyewitness account and is recorded in Acts 2. On that Shavuot morning, God initiated a new covenant with Israel as He foretold: "Behold, the days are coming, says the LORD, when I will make a *new* covenant with the house of Israel" (Jer. 31:31). On that morning He poured out His Holy Spirit as He also foretold: "'The Redeemer [Messiah] will come to Zion, And to those who turn from transgression [by repentance] in Jacob,' Says the LORD. 'As for Me,' says the LORD, 'this is My covenant with them: *My Spirit who is upon you*'" (Isa. 59:20-21).

But even as that promise was for them, it is also for you. Call upon the name of the Lord, and you will be saved.

ראש השנה

"'And in the seventh month, on the first day of the month, you shall have a holy convocation. You shall do no customary work. For you it is a day of blowing the trumpets'" (Num. 29:1).

Rosh Hashanah — The Feast of Trumpets

Kevin L. Howard

It is not uncommon for holidays to have musical instruments incorporated into their celebration. Rarely, however, is the sum and substance of a holiday's celebration solely dependent upon a musical instrument. Yet, such was the case with Israel's fifth holy day, known as *Rosh Hashanah*.

■■■■■■ THE BIBLICAL OBSERVANCE

The Meaning of Rosh Hashanah

Although Rosh Hashanah has its roots firmly planted in the Bible, it is never known by that name in Scripture. Instead, it is referred to as *Zikhron Teruah* ("Memorial of Blowing [of trumpets]," Lev. 23:24) and *Yom Teruah* ("Day of Blowing [of trumpets]," Num. 29:1). Based upon these biblical designations, the ancient observance of Rosh Hashanah is often simply referred to as "the Feast of Trumpets," a day of sounding trumpets in the Temple and throughout the land of Israel.

Rosh Hashanah literally means "Head of the Year." However, this designation was not applied to this feast until at least the second century A.D., more than 1,500 years after the institution of the holiday. Following the A.D. 70 destruction of the Temple, its observance was radically altered. For the holiday, it was a matter of survival in the midst of a tragic situation. Continued observance of the Feast of Trumpets was threatened due to the absence of the Temple and its sacrificial system. As a result, synagogue liturgy was enlarged, new traditions were suggested, and emphases were shifted in an attempt to preserve and adapt the observance of this holiday for a people scattered outside their homeland and stripped of their Temple.

The timing of the ancient Feast of Trumpets coincided with the beginning of Israel's civil New Year. After the A.D. 70 destruction of the second Temple, the two observances became inseparably connected. In time, the Feast of Trumpets was largely overshadowed and assimilated by the Jewish New Year, becoming known as *Rosh Hashanah* ("The Head of the Year").

The Time of Rosh Hashanah

Rosh Hashanah is observed in the autumn of the year. On the Hebrew calendar, Rosh Hashanah occurs on the first day of Tishri, the seventh Hebrew month (usually mid-September to early October). Israel's two other autumn holidays occur only days later: Yom Kippur (Day of Atonement) on Tishri 10 and the Feast of Tabernacles beginning on Tishri 15.

In the Bible, the Feast of Trumpets was celebrated as a one-day holiday. For the Diaspora (Jewish communities living outside the land of Israel), many holidays were and still are celebrated for an additional day. The reason is rooted in the uncertainty of the Jewish calendar. The beginning of each Hebrew month was originally dependent upon the sighting of the New Moon. The precise timing of the New Moon was not always easily determined due to clouds or a lack of witnesses. Rosh Hashanah greatly compounded the problem since it fell upon the first day of the month, the actual New Moon, making it especially difficult to notify Jewish communities that the holiday had, in fact, already begun. To decrease the chance for error, Rosh Hashanah was observed for two days, a tradition which continues even in Israel today.

The Record of Rosh Hashanah

The biblical record for Rosh Hashanah observance is neither lengthy nor complicated. Israel was simply commanded to memorialize the day by blowing trumpets and to keep the day as a sabbath of rest (Lev. 23:23-25; Num. 29:1).

The biblical record concerning the Temple sacrifices is equally straight-forward (Num. 29:2-6). A special burnt offering was offered on Rosh Hashanah consisting of a young bull, a ram, and seven lambs. A kid goat was also sacrificed as a sin offering. Both of these offerings were in addition to the required daily sacrifices (Num. 28:1-8) and those for the new moon (Num. 28:11-15) which were also offered on that day.

The actual observance of the Feast of Trumpets is recorded only once in Scripture. Ezra, the scribe, related that it was during the Feast of Trumpets that the Temple altar was rebuilt, and sacrifices were reinstituted by those who returned from Babylonian exile (Ezra 3:1-6). Nehemiah recorded that sweeping revival also took place in Israel that same day as Ezra rehearsed God's law in the ears of the people (Neh. 7:73-8:13).

The Importance of Rosh Hashanah

In relationship to the New Moon, Rosh Hashanah is unique. It is the only Jewish holiday which occurs on the first day of the month, at the New Moon, when the moon is dark and only a thin crescent. All other Jewish holidays occur later in their respective months when the moon is bright.

Even as the seventh *day* and the seventh *year* were holy under Mosaic law (Ex. 20:8-10; Lev. 25:4), so, too, was Tishri, the seventh *month*. Significantly, Rosh Hashanah occurs on the first day of this sabbath of months in which all three of Israel's autumn holidays occur. In ancient Israel, the New Moon was normally announced by short blasts of the trumpet, but the New Moon of the seventh month was celebrated by long blasts, emphasizing its solemnity and uniqueness among months.

The Instrument of Rosh Hashanah

The Types of Trumpets

Most English Bibles do not clearly distinguish the different types of Hebrew trumpets. The *hatzotzerah* was a straight metal trumpet that was flared at the end. God commanded the sons of Israel to fashion two silver trumpets "of hammered work" (Num. 10:1-2). The priests sounded these silver trumpets over the sacrifices as a memorial to the Lord (Num. 10:10). In Solomon's day, the number of silver trumpets in the Temple had grown to a magnificent ensemble of 120 trumpets (2 Chr. 5:12). According to Josephus, the Jewish historian, the priests also blew this trumpet from the southwest corner of the Temple wall to announce the beginning and ending of every Sabbath (*Wars of the Jews* 4.9.12). Renderings of these silver trumpets have been uncovered archaeologically with depictions of them found on the victory arch of Titus in Rome (A.D. 70) and on silver coins minted during the Simon Bar Kochba revolt (A.D. 132-135). In recent days, these trumpets have been reconstructed by the Temple Institute in Jerusalem in preparation for the future rebuilding of the Temple.

The other Hebrew trumpet, a *shofar*, was a curved trumpet fashioned from a ram's horn. In the Hebrew language, the *shofar* ("ram's horn trumpet") was clearly distinguished from a *keren*, "the horn of an animal," when not used as a musical instrument. Trumpets constructed from cows' horns were rejected due to the reminder of Israel's idolatrous worship of the golden calf in the wilderness. The ram's horn was seen as a much more pleasant reminder of God's deliverance of Isaac through the ram caught by its horns in the thicket.

When Scripture designated Tishri 1 as a "day of blowing" and a "memorial of blowing," the type of trumpet for Rosh Hashanah was not specifically identified. Almost without exception, historical observance and rabbinic tradition specified the *shofar* ("ram's horn"), not the silver trumpets of the priests, as the primary instrument intended by Scripture.

Perhaps the original reason for specifying the ram's horn is to be found in the announcement of the Jubilee Year. Scripture designated the *shofar* ("ram's horn"), not the trumpet fashioned from precious metal, as the trumpet to be blown on Yom Kippur (Lev. 25:9). Every fiftieth year, this shofar announced the arrival of the Jubilee Year in which the slaves were freed and the fields were given rest from the farming cycle. The modern custom of sounding the shofar at the end of Yom Kippur preserves this ancient command even though Jubilee years are no longer reckoned.

The Types of Blasts

After the destruction of the Temple, much debate arose among the rabbis concerning the sounding of the shofar since Scripture did not explicitly describe the manner of blasts required. A compromise was reached that covered all possibilities. The *tekiah* was defined as a long, unwavering blast. The *shevarim* were defined as three short, broken blasts. The *teruah* mentioned in Scripture was declared to be a nine-part staccato blast somewhat reminiscent of sobbing. Collectively, the following pattern was developed for blowing the shofar: a long blast (*tekiah*) — three short blasts (*shevarim*) — nine staccato blasts (*teruah*) — one long blast (*tekiah*).

The Types of Uses

Apart from the sacrificial ceremony, the trumpet had several major uses for the nation of Israel: It *gathered an assembly before the Lord* (Num. 10:2-4), and it *sounded a battle alarm* (Num. 10:9; cf. Jud. 3:27; 7:19-22;

Neh. 4:18-22; Ezek. 33:3-6). The shofar also *announced the coronation of a new king* as in the cases of Solomon (1 Ki. 1:34, 39), Jehu (2 Ki. 9:13), Joash (2 Ki. 11:12-14), and the treacherous Absalom (2 Sam. 15:10).

In June 1967, the haunting sound of the shofar again echoed on Jerusalem's Temple Mount after almost 1,900 years. It was sounded by Chief Rabbi Shlomo Goren after Israeli soldiers restored Jewish sovereignty over East Jerusalem and reunited Israel's eternal capital.

The Service of Rosh Hashanah

In the days of Israel's Temple, the silver trumpets were sounded for the burnt offerings or peace offerings. This was in harmony with the Mosaic command: "You shall blow the trumpets over your burnt offerings and over the sacrifices of your peace offerings" (Num. 10:10). As the sacrifices were brought and offered on the altar , the silver trumpets were blown by the priests, a fact historically confirmed by Scripture (2 Chr. 29:27-28) and by Josephus (*Antiquities of the Jews* 3.12.6).

On the Feast of Trumpets, an additional priest was employed to sound a shofar. He stood in the row of priests with the silver trumpets facing the altar. The shofar sounded long, sustained blasts while the silver trumpets sounded short blasts over the sacrifices of the day.

More than one hundred priests officiated during the Feast of Trumpets due to the many morning, evening, new moon, and festival sacrifices. As the festive drink offerings were poured on the altar, the levitical choir sang Psalm 81, the Feast of Trumpets psalm: "Blow the trumpet at the time of the New Moon, At the full moon, on our solemn feast day. For this is a statute for Israel, A law of the God of Jacob" (Ps. 81:3-4).

■ ▰▰▰ THE MODERN OBSERVANCE

Rosh Hashanah's modern observance bears, at best, only a remote resemblance to the biblical Feast of Trumpets. The holiday's very name change indicates that it has been recast with many traditions superimposed over the biblical observance.

The Days of Awe

In Jewish tradition, the ten-day period from Rosh Hashanah to Yom Kippur (the two high holy days of Judaism) is called the "Days of Awe." Jewish tradition holds that, during this ten-day period, divine judgment is rendered to determine whether a person will continue to live or die in the coming year. It is believed that God reviews the books of judgment on Rosh Hashanah (Tishri 1) and metes out final judgment on Yom Kippur (Tishri 10). These ten days are believed to be the last chance to repent before God's judgment is finalized for the coming year.

According to Jewish tradition, three books are opened on Rosh Hashanah: the Book of Life for the wicked, the Book of Life for the righteous, and the Book of Life for the in-between. As the Judge of the Universe reviews mankind's deeds of the past year, He inscribes the name of every individual in one of these books. Judgment against the wicked is final and irrevocable; they will have life cut short in the coming year. Those recorded in the book of the righteous will be mercifully granted another year of life and prosperity by the Lord. For the remainder (those not written in either of these books), the sealing of their fate is deferred and hangs in the balance until Yom Kippur. If they sincerely repent during the Days of Awe, tradition holds that God will grant them life until the following Yom Kippur. Reflecting this tradition, the common greeting during the Days of Awe is *"Leshanah tovah tikatevu"* ("May you be inscribed [in the Book of Life] for a good year!").

This judgment-book tradition, although greatly embellished, finds its origin in Scripture. King David penned the words, "Let them be blotted out of the book of the living, And not be written with the righteous" (Ps. 69:28). The prophet Moses pleaded: "'Yet now, if You will forgive their sin— but if not, I pray, blot me out of Your book which You have written.' And the LORD said to Moses, 'Whoever has sinned against Me, I will blot him out of My book'" (Ex. 32:32-33).

Because the "Days of Awe" are such a solemn time of self-examination, joyful activities are usually forbidden. Weddings and other festive occasions are postponed until after Yom Kippur.

Prayers of Repentance

The week before Rosh Hashanah is usually marked by the recitation of penitential prayers called *Selihot* ("forgivenesses"). These heart-rending prayers for forgiveness are in preparation for the Days of Awe and customarily begin at midnight the Saturday night before Rosh Hashanah.

The Casting Ceremony

The Rosh Hashanah ceremony known as *Tashlikh* ("cast off") symbolizes self-purification and the shedding of one's sins. It arose during the Middle Ages and is still widely observed today. On the afternoon of the first day of Rosh Hashanah, observant Jews congregate near a body of water such as the ocean, a river, or even a well, to recite the Tashlikh prayer. In Israel, thousands of worshipers, with prayer book in hand and dressed in their holiday attire, can be seen on the beaches of the Mediterranean or in Jerusalem at the Pool of Siloam, reciting the Tashlikh prayer on Rosh Hashanah. The brief Tashlikh prayer is composed of several Hebrew Scriptures in the following order: Micah 7:18-20, Psalm 118:5-9, Psalm 33, Psalm 130, and often Isaiah 11:9. The ceremony itself takes its name from the Hebrew Scripture in the prayer, "You will cast [*tashlikh*] all our sins Into the depths of the sea" (Mic. 7:19). After the prayer, worshipers will often shake their pockets or cast bread crumbs into the water. This action symbolically rids them of clinging sins so that their sin may be carried away and remembered no more.

The Shofar

Rosh Hashanah was often referred to as *Yom Ha-Din* ("Judgment Day") by the rabbis since it began the Days of Awe, the traditional time of God's judgment. Consequently, repentance has always been foremost in the Jewish mind at this time.

Beginning with the sabbath before the new moon of the sixth Hebrew month and continuing throughout the month, the shofar is blown every morning after the *Shakharit* (morning prayer service). It serves as a call to repentance and a solemn reminder that the most awesome holy days on the Jewish calendar are approaching.

Both Jewish and Christian theology view Satan (Hebrew for "adversary") as the great enemy of God and His people. In the Bible, Satan is often seen in the role as an accuser of God's people (Job 1:6-2:7; Zech. 3:1; Rev. 12:10). Jewish tradition teaches that, on Rosh Hashanah, Satan appears before the Almighty to accuse Israel as the books for judgment are opened. The ancient rabbis, therefore, suggested the traditional purpose for the shofar on Rosh Hashanah: "Why do they blow [the shofar]? . . . in order to confound Satan" (Rosh Hashanah 16a). They believed that the many blasts of the shofar on Rosh Hashanah would confuse Satan, leading him to believe that the Messiah had arrived and his authority had ended. Based upon this tradition, it is customary to sound a total of 100 shofar blasts on each day of the Rosh Hashanah synagogue services.

Synagogue Liturgy

Synagogue services for Rosh Hashanah are some of the longest of the year, surpassed only by those of Yom Kippur. It is not unusual for the lengthy morning services to continue for five or more hours.

The synagogue liturgy of prayers and readings for Rosh Hashanah is built around the theme of God's kingship. For two thousand years, the Rosh Hashanah liturgy has been structured around three Hebrew benedictions: *Malkhiyot* ("Kingships"), *Zikhronot* ("Remembrances"), and *Shofarot* ("Rams' horns"). After each benediction, the melancholy blast of the shofar is heard: one long blast, three short blasts, nine staccato blasts, and one final sustained blast.

The *Malkhiyot* emphasizes *God's majesty* and His lofty position as Sovereign King of the universe as it proclaims: "May all the inhabitants of the world realize and know that to thee every knee must bend, every tongue must vow allegiance . . . . The Lord shall be King forever and ever."

The *Zikhronot* testifies of *God's remembrance* of His everlasting covenant with Israel as it pleads: "Remember in our behalf, Lord our God, the covenant, the kindness, and the solemn promise which thou didst make to our father Abraham on Mount Moriah."

The *Shofarot* focuses upon the *key role of the shofar* in the history of the nation. It speaks of Mt. Sinai where the Lord first revealed Himself with the sound of the shofar: "The whole world trembled at thy presence, creation shook in awe before thee, when thou, our King, didst reveal thyself on Mount Sinai . . . amid the blasting of the shofar didst thou appear to them."

The benediction also speaks of the end of days when God will again reveal Himself through fire and the sounding of the shofar as He sends the Messiah: "The Lord shall appear over them; his arrow shall go forth like lightning. The Lord God shall sound the shofar and march amid the storms of the south" (cf. Zech. 9:14).

Because of the inseparable connection between the shofar and Rosh Hashanah, the assigned synagogue reading for the second day of Rosh Hashanah is Genesis 22 where Abraham bound Isaac on the sacrificial altar. In this great passage the Lord provided the substitutionary ram in the place of Isaac.

The Jewish New Year

In spite of the solemn introspection and the focus on repentance, Rosh Hashanah has its joyful side. Since Rosh Hashanah is identified with the civil New Year, it is also a time of happiness. It is customary to send colorful New Year greeting cards to friends and family on Rosh Hashanah, wishing them the universal Hebrew greeting *Shanah tovah* ("A good year").

Traditional Foods

Rosh Hashanah, like so many other holidays, has acquired its own set of traditional foods. The most widespread tradition is that of dipping apples in honey. This tradition expresses the desire for sweetness in the coming year.

At the evening meal of the second night of Rosh Hashanah, it is customary to wear a new outfit and to eat a sweet fruit which one has not eaten in a long time. Observant Jews will often deny themselves apples, grapes, or pomegranates throughout the summer so that they may eat them with increased enjoyment on Rosh Hashanah.

Two oval loaves of braided *hallah* bread are usually found on the weekly Sabbath table. On Rosh Hashanah, it is customary to eat *round* loaves of hallah bread, symbolizing crowns, as a reminder of the synagogue liturgy's emphasis upon God's kingship.

The Birthday of the World

In the Talmud, the ancient rabbinical commentary suggested, "In the month of Tishri the world was created" (Rosh Hashanah 10b). Other rabbinic authorities suggested that Rosh Hashanah was not only the birthday of the world, but the very day on which man was created, making it the beginning of the day of man.

 THE FUTURE FULFILLMENT

Like Israel's other feasts, the Feast of Trumpets carries strong prophetic overtones. However, this holy day commemorates no historical events, but portrays future events for the nation. The Feast of Trumpets is next on Israel's prophetic calendar. Israel's four springtime holidays (Passover, Unleavened Bread, Firstfruits, and the Feast of Weeks) were fulfilled in connection with the Messiah's first coming. Israel's three autumn holidays (Feast of Trumpets, Yom Kippur, and Tabernacles) will be fulfilled at His second coming. The ancient rabbis held a similar view: "In the month of

Nisan [at Passover], our ancestors were redeemed, and in Tishri [Rosh Hashanah], they will be redeemed in the time to come" (Rosh Hashanah 11a).

Israel's Dark Day

The Feast of Trumpets is Israel's dark day. It occurs at the New Moon when the primary night light of the heavens is darkened. Israel's prophets repeatedly warned of a coming dark day of judgment. They knew it as "the Day of the Lord," that terrible period of time at the end of this age when the Lord will pour out His fiery judgment. The Day of the Lord will be a time when the Lord pours out His wrath not only upon Israel's enemies, but upon Israel herself to bring her to repentance and into the New Covenant.

The prophet Amos spoke of this dark day of judgment: "Woe to you who desire the day of the LORD! For what good is the day of the LORD to you? It will be darkness, and not light. It will be as though a man fled from a lion, And a bear met him! Or as though he went into the house, Leaned his hand on the wall, And a serpent bit him! Is not the day of the LORD darkness, and not light? Is it not very dark, with no brightness in it?" (Amos 5:18-20).

The Hebrew prophet Zephaniah penned the ominous warning: "The great day of the LORD is near . . . . That day is a day of wrath, A day of trouble and distress, A day of devastation and desolation, A day of darkness and gloominess, A day of clouds and thick darkness, A day of trumpet . . ." (Zeph. 1:14-16).

But even as the darkening of the moon in the night heavens announced the Feast of Trumpets, so, too, the heavens will be divinely darkened in a future day as the Day of the Lord commences. Joel revealed: "The sun shall be turned into darkness, And the moon into blood, *Before* the coming of the great and awesome day of the LORD" (Joel 2:31; cf. Isa. 13:9-10; 34:4, 8; Joel 3:15; Acts 2:20).

The apostle John also described this cosmic disturbance and darkness which will announce the Day of the Lord: "I looked when He opened the sixth seal, and behold, there was a great earthquake; and the sun became black as sackcloth of hair, and the moon became like blood. And the stars of heaven fell to the earth . . . . For the great day of His wrath has come, and who is able to stand?" (Rev. 6:12-17).

The day is coming in which the Lord will switch off the natural lights of heaven. He will then pour out His wrath with relentless fury upon this wicked world as the Messiah returns to set up His kingdom. It will be Israel's darkest day, her "Days of Awe," as God's wrath prepares her for repentance, even her national Day of Atonement.

The Last Trump

Scripture often speaks of men or angels blowing trumpets, yet only twice is it recorded that *God* blows a trumpet. In both instances, it is the shofar.

The first occasion was at Mt. Sinai when the Lord revealed Himself from Heaven and prepared to bring the nation under the Old Covenant. The Shekinah glory of the Lord descended with a fiery tempest and the sound of the shofar: "Now Mount Sinai was completely in smoke, because the LORD descended upon it in fire . . . . And when the blast of the trumpet sounded long and became louder and louder, Moses spoke, and God answered him by voice. Then the LORD came down upon Mount Sinai" (Ex. 19:18-20).

The last occasion on which the Lord will blow the shofar will be at the Messiah's return. The Lord will once again descend from Heaven with the whirlwind, the clouds of His glory fire, and the sound of the trumpet. The prophet Zechariah predicted: "Then the LORD will be seen over them, And His arrow will go forth like lightning. The Lord GOD will blow the trumpet, And go with whirlwinds from the south" (Zech. 9:14).

The ancient rabbis repeatedly quoted this verse in connection with the coming of the Messiah: "And it is the ram's horn that the Holy One, blessed be he, is destined to blow when the son of David, our righteous one, will reveal himself, as it is said: 'And the Lord God will blow the horn'" (Tanna debe Eliyahu Zutta XXII).

As the Day of the Lord begins, God's last trump will be sounded, the Messiah will reveal Himself in great wrath, and He will prepare the nation to be brought into the New Covenant (Jer. 31:31; Ezek. 20:35-38; Zech. 13:9).

Ancient Jewish tradition held that the resurrection of the dead would occur on Rosh Hashanah. Reflecting this tradition, Jewish gravestones were often engraved with a shofar.

Both of these great events — God's last trump and the resurrection of the righteous — are intricately connected to the Rapture of the Church in the New Testament. Paul revealed: "Behold, I tell you a mystery: We shall not all sleep, but we shall all be changed — in a moment, in the twinkling of an eye, at the *last trumpet*. For the trumpet will sound, and the dead will be raised incorruptible, and we shall be changed" (1 Cor. 15:51-52).

In another letter, Paul described the Lord's coming: "For the Lord Himself will descend from heaven with a shout, with the voice of an archangel, and with the *trumpet of God*. And the dead in Christ will rise first. Then we who are alive and remain shall be caught up together with them in the clouds to meet the Lord in the air. And thus we shall always be with the Lord" (1 Th. 4:16-17).

The day is coming in which the Lord who sits on Heaven's throne will again descend in the fiery clouds of His Shekinah glory. Jesus referred to this as His "coming on the clouds of heaven with power and great glory" (Mt. 24:30). God's last trump will be blown, and the Day of the Lord will begin. Like Israel's ancient trumpet, God's last trump will accomplish several purposes. First, it will *gather an assembly to the Lord* in what is known as "the Rapture of the Church." The righteous will be delivered "from the wrath to come" (1 Th. 1:10) since God has not appointed them unto wrath (1 Th. 5:9). The righteous dead will be resurrected, and the living will be gathered "from the four winds" (Mt. 24:31). Second, the last trump will *sound God's battle alarm* against Satan and this wicked world as He begins "the great day of His wrath" (Rev. 6:17). This will draw the day of man's rebellion to a close. Finally, the last trump will *announce the coming and soon coronation of the Messiah*, for He alone will be "exalted in that day" (Isa. 2:17).

 # THE APPLICATION

National repentance by Israel is a prerequisite to the Messiah's return. Israel's repentance is one of the chief purposes of the Day of the Lord. Israel's King will not return to her until she is ready to receive Him. The rabbis of old correctly understood the prophets when they declared: "Were Israel to practice repentance for even one day, they would be redeemed, and the Branch of David [the Messiah] would come" (Song of Songs Rabbah 5:2).

Tragically, unrepentant Israel (along with the Gentiles) will suffer the fury of God's wrath before she is willing to say, "Blessed is he [Jesus the Messiah] who comes in the name of the LORD" (Ps. 118:26; cf. Mt. 23:39).

But the concept of repentance is far more basic to God's Word than just its connection to prophecy. Repentance is required of all men. Repentance is the *life and death* principle in Scripture: "The soul who sins shall die . . . But if a wicked man turns from all his sins . . . he shall surely live"

(Ezek. 18:20-21).

Known as *teshuvah* in Hebrew, repentance literally means "to return"; that is, to return to God. It involves a reversal in spiritual direction and is accomplished by two actions.

On the one hand, repentance requires that an individual *turn away from sin* by forsaking it. The Almighty beckons: "Repent, and turn from all your transgressions, so that iniquity will not be your ruin. Cast away from you all the transgressions which you have committed" (Ezek. 18:30-31).

On the other hand, repentance requires that an individual *turn toward God* by putting complete trust in Him and His Redeemer, the Messiah. King David wrote: "Kiss the Son [the Messiah], lest He be angry, And you perish in the way, When His wrath is kindled but a little. Blessed are all those who put their trust in Him" (Ps. 2:12).

It is to this same great King over all the earth that "every knee shall bow" and "every tongue shall take an oath" (Isa. 45:23). There is no other way to come to God.

The day is coming in which the Messiah King will come. Jesus will return to Jerusalem. He will reign over all the earth. He will reign forever, even as the prophets foretold. But not all will enter His glorious kingdom. When the Redeemer comes to Zion, He will come "to those who turn from transgression" (Isa. 59:20) and to those who "put their trust in Him" (Ps. 2:12).

Rabbi Eliezer, one of Israel's ancient rabbis, declared, "Repent one day before your death." His astonished disciples asked, "Does then one know on what day he will die?" The rabbi replied, "Then all the more reason that he repent today" (Shabbat 153a). The idea is, of course, that men do not know when they will die; thus, repentance is urgent. The voice of Scripture is in strong agreement. Today is the day of repentance. We do not know the number of our days nor the day of His wrath. We must seek Him now while the gates of repentance remain open, as the prophet implored, "Seek the LORD while He may be found, Call upon Him while He is near" (Isa. 55:6).

Have you truly repented? Have you turned away from your sin and toward God, and thereby passed from death unto life? To those who do, He faithfully promises to "cast all their sins into the depths of the sea" and remember them no more.

YOM KIPPUR

יום כפור

"Also the tenth day of this seventh month shall
be the Day of Atonement. It shall be a holy convocation
for you; you shall afflict your souls" (Lev. 23:27).

Yom Kippur – The Day of Atonement

Kevin L. Howard

Israel's most awesome holy day, known as *Yom Kippur* or "The Day of Atonement," is an ever-present theme woven throughout the pages of Scripture. Three and one-half millennia after its divine institution, Yom Kippur still wields a powerful influence over the culture and worship of Israel. But of even greater import, Yom Kippur provides a necessary backdrop for understanding the scope of the Messiah's payment for sin and the security of God's people today.

■ ■ THE BIBLICAL OBSERVANCE

The Meaning of Yom Kippur

"The Day of Atonement" is the English equivalent for *Yom Kippur*. For many, however, the word "atonement" is vague and sheds no light on the meaning of the holiday. *Kippur* is from the Hebrew word *kaphar* meaning "to cover." Therefore, the word *atonement* simply means a *covering*.

It was on Yom Kippur that an atonement (covering) was made for the previous year's sins. The atonement or covering consisted of a blood sacrifice of an innocent animal. The Lord commanded, "'For the life of the flesh is in the blood, and I have given it to you upon the altar to make atonement (covering) for your souls; for it is the blood that makes atonement (covering) for the soul'" (Lev. 17:11).

The Time of Yom Kippur

Yom Kippur, Israel's sixth divinely instituted holy day, occurs in the autumn of the year. On the Hebrew calendar, it falls on the tenth day of Tishri, the seventh Hebrew month, which roughly corresponds to September or October. It is observed between two other major biblical holidays: the Feast of Trumpets (known as *Rosh Hashanah* today) on Tishri 1, and the Feast of Tabernacles which begins on Tishri 15.

The Record of Yom Kippur

Three separate passages outline the biblical observance of Yom Kippur. Divine instructions were given for the high priest (Lev. 16), for the people (Lev. 23:26-32), and for the sacrifices (Num. 29:7-11).

The Importance of Yom Kippur

Yom Kippur was the most solemn day of the year for the *people* of Israel. It was often simply referred to as "the Day." Yom Kippur was designated by the Lord as a day in which "you shall afflict your souls" (Lev. 23:27, 32). By definition this was understood to mean fasting (cf. Ezra 8:21). It was a day devoted to fasting and repenting of one's sins during the past year. Yom Kippur was not the only fast within Judaism, but it was the only fast mandated by Scripture. The Israelite who failed to devote himself to fasting and repentance on Yom Kippur was to be "cut off from his people" (Lev. 23:29). Yom Kippur was also a day with prohibitions against all forms of work. Those who likewise chose to ignore this regulation would suffer the death penalty (Lev. 23:30).

Yom Kippur was also a very solemn day for the *priesthood* of Israel. Only on that singular day of the year was the high priest permitted to enter the Holy of Holies in the Temple and stand before the presence of God's glory. In doing so, the high priest was required to wear holy garments woven from white linen instead of his normal colorful garments overlaid with the golden breastplate. His linen garments were worn only on that day and never again.

The solemnity of Yom Kippur was further emphasized by the increased number of animal *sacrifices*. Besides the regular, daily burnt offerings with their required grain and drink offerings, additional burnt offerings were made. These additional offerings included a bull, a ram, and seven lambs for the people, and a ram for the priesthood (Num. 29:7-11).

The Service of Yom Kippur

The Preparation

It was absolutely crucial to the nation that their high priest did not inadvertently become ritually unclean and thereby disqualified from performing his Yom Kippur duties. To safeguard against this disastrous possibility, the high priest was required to leave his home one week before Yom Kippur to stay in the high priest's quarters inside the Temple area. During the week, the high priest was twice sprinkled with the ashes of a red heifer to circumvent the possibility that he had become unclean through touching a dead body. Such was the normal cleansing process for ceremonial defilement (Num. 19:1-10).

A substitute was also appointed for the high priest in the event he should die or, despite all precautions, become unclean. This substitute was usually next in line for the high priest's office and, as such, the most powerful individual in the Temple after the high priest. He was the captain of the Temple (Acts 4:1; 5:24, 26) and exercised direct command of the officers of the Temple guard (Levites who patrolled the Temple facilities, enforcing Mosaic law).

The high priest did not perform the Temple services on a regular basis, but during the week leading up to Yom Kippur, he alone conducted the sacrifices. All aspects of his duties for the coming holy day were faithfully practiced, whether it was sprinkling blood with his thumb and forefinger, burning incense, lighting the menorah (lampstand), or rehearsing his movements throughout the Temple. There could be no mistakes, or the result would be a monumental catastrophe and humiliation for the nation — Israel's sacrifices would be disqualified, leaving the sins of the people uncovered.

The Morning Service

Although the Jewish day began at sunset, the Temple service for Yom Kippur did not begin until dawn the next morning. The ashes on the altar were cleared away, and four fires instead of the normal three were lit to set the day apart as distinct.

On any other day, the high priest would merely wash his hands and feet with water from the priestly laver **ⓐ** before performing his service. On Yom Kippur, he was required to totally immerse himself in a special golden bath **ⓑ** near the Court of the Priests. This was carried out behind a large linen curtain which revealed only the shadow of his movements to the public view. This assured that no changes were made to the required procedures.

The high priest put on his golden garments with great care. His majestic purple robe was hemmed with tiny golden bells so that the people could hear him work as he represented them. Over the top of his robe, he wore a golden breastplate which was studded with twelve precious stones — a constant reminder that he was the representative of the twelve tribes of Israel before the true and living God.

After dressing, the high priest washed his hands and feet to perform the regular daily service. Following the morning service, the high priest returned to his bath chamber **ⓑ** to change into his white linen garments for Yom Kippur. Five times during the day he changed clothing, and five times he followed the same cleansing procedure. Each time, he washed his hands and feet, removed his garments, totally immersed his body, put on his change of clothing, and washed his hands and feet a second time.

The Afternoon Service

The afternoon Temple service was the main focus of the Yom Kippur observance. Through the sacrifices of this service, atonement was made for the sins of the priesthood and people of Israel for the preceding year.

The Confession of the High Priest

The high priest began the afternoon service by moving to the Court of the Priests where a young bull awaited him **ⓒ** between the altar and the Temple porch. Since this bull was the sin offering for the high priest and the priesthood, the ceremony took place near the Temple where the priests ministered. The high priest would press his two hands upon the head of the young bull, as a sign of identification with it as his substitute, and make a confession of his sin. Three times during his confession, he would pronounce the covenant name of the Lord (*YHWH*). (Under Jewish oral law, this holy name was forbidden to be spoken on any other occasion lest it be taken in vain [Ex. 20:7] by mispronouncing it or misusing it.) Each time the name was uttered by the high priest, the people and the priests would fall on their faces in worship and repeat, "Blessed be

His name whose glorious kingdom is forever and ever!"

The Two Goats

The high priest was next escorted by two priests to the eastern side of the altar **e**. On his right was the deputy high priest (the priest appointed to take his place in case he became unable to fulfill his duties). On his left, he was escorted by the chief priest of the division of priests chosen to minister that week. In all, the priesthood was divided into twenty-four courses of priests, with each course serving one week on a rotating 24-week schedule (1 Chr. 24:1-19).

Two goats stood there, side by side, awaiting the high priest. They were identical in size, color, and value. They faced the Temple and gazed at the high priest and his entourage as they approached.

Two golden lots were placed inside a golden vessel sitting on the stone pavement nearby. One was inscribed with "for *YHWH*" and the other with "for *azazel*." The high priest shook the vessel and randomly took one lot in each hand. As he held the lots to the foreheads of the goats and determined the outcome, he declared them "a sin offering to the Lord." The two goats together were viewed as one singular offering.

The goat upon which the lot "for *azazel*" fell was immediately identified by a crimson strip of wool tied to one of its horns. It was then turned around to face the people whose sin would later be placed on its head.

Some debate exists as to the exact meaning of *azazel*. Some believe it was a reference to Satan, for in Jewish tradition *Azazel* was the name of a fallen angel. However, most scholars believe that the word was derived from the Hebrew word *azel* which carries the idea of "escape." This line of thought led to calling this goat the "scapegoat" since it escaped death and was instead driven into the wilderness.

The goat determined "for *YHWH*" was left to face the large stone altar, the place where it was shortly to be offered as a sin offering.

The Sin Offering for the Priesthood

The high priest returned to the young bull **c** a second time and pressed his hands on its head. This time he confessed the sins of the priesthood, whereas before he had confessed only his own sin upon its head.

123

The bull was then slaughtered by the high priest and its blood collected in a golden bowl. A nearby attending priest was handed the bowl and given the task of stirring the blood so that it would not congeal.

Burning the Incense

Next, the high priest took a golden fire pan or censer and walked up the ramp to the altar **e**. He carefully filled the fire pan with live coals from the fires burning on top of the altar. Then he took two handfuls of incense and placed them in a golden ladle. With the fire pan in his right hand and the incense in his left, he ascended to the Temple and passed through the Holy Place **f** where the lampstand, table of showbread, and altar of incense were located. At the rear of the Holy Place, he paused to make his way through the veil (the thick curtain which separated the Holy Place from the Holy of Holies). Once inside the Holy of Holies, **g** he stood in quiet solitude. Only the soft orange glow of the coals lit the room.

The high priest poured the incense onto the coals and waited a few moments for a fragrant cloud of smoke to fill the room before making his way back through the thick curtain.

In Solomon's Temple, the Ark of the Covenant resided in the Holy of Holies, and the Shekinah glory of the Lord rested above it. After the Babylonian captivity, the Ark was never recovered. The Holy of Holies remained an empty room with only a singular stone (called the "foundation stone") projecting up from the pavement three fingers in height (2 $^1/_4$ inches).

Sprinkling the Blood

The high priest then took the golden bowl filled with the bull's blood and returned to the Holy of Holies **g**. He carefully sprinkled the blood before the Ark of the Covenant. He sprinkled it once upwards and then seven times downwards as though he were cracking a whip. All the while he counted aloud to prevent any errors. He then exited the Holy of Holies and placed the bowl in a golden stand.

The high priest continued outside to the Court of the Priests **c** to slaughter the goat set aside for the Lord. He collected its blood in a golden bowl and entered the Holy of Holies a third time, sprinkling the blood of the goat in the same manner as that of the bull.

Afterwards, he sprinkled the outside of the veil with the blood of the bull. Then he repeated this procedure with the blood of the goat. Finally, he poured the two bowls together and sprinkled the horns (protruding points on each corner) of the altar **e** in the courtyard.

The Scapegoat

Attention was then drawn to the remaining goat as it stood in the afternoon sun, nervously twitching its ears and staring at the congregation. The high priest proceeded to lay his hands on its head and confessed the sins of the people upon it. The scapegoat was then led through the Eastern Gate by a priest more than ten miles into the wilderness, never to be seen again.

In the days of the Second Temple, the scapegoat was actually killed so that it (carrying Israel's sins) could not wander into an inhabited place at a later time. To prevent the possibility of such a tragedy, the scapegoat was led to the edge of a rocky crag and pushed off backwards by the priest.

While the scapegoat was being led into the wilderness and the people awaited word that it had been accomplished, the afternoon service continued. The high priest finished sacrificing the bull and the goat on the altar, and their remaining parts were taken outside the city to be burned.

Then the high priest addressed the people. He read the Yom Kippur passages from Leviticus and quoted the Numbers passage by heart to verify that all commandments had been duly accomplished.

Finally, the remaining offerings for Yom Kippur were offered. These were the burnt offerings, as opposed to the sin offerings.

With the warm afternoon sun setting in the west and the shadows growing long, the high priest entered the Holy of Holies **g** a final time to remove the fire pan and incense ladle. He then bathed for the fifth time during the day and changed into his golden garments. As the cool autumn night quickly approached, he performed the regular evening Temple service and drew Yom Kippur to a close.

THE MODERN OBSERVANCE

Jewish Tradition

The modern observance of Yom Kippur bears very little resemblance to its biblical observance. Modern observance is based more upon the traditions of men than upon the pattern established in God's law.

This is largely due to the influence of one man, Rabbi Yohanan ben Zakkai, the well-known rabbi during the days of the Roman destruction of the Temple. Jewish history records:

> As Rabban Yohanan ben Zakkai was coming forth from Jerusalem, Rabbi Joshua followed after him and beheld the Temple in ruins. "Woe unto us!" Rabbi Joshua cried, "that this, the place where the iniquities of Israel were atoned for is laid waste!" "My son," Rabban Yohanan said to him, "be not grieved; we have another atonement as effective as this. And what is it? It is acts of loving-kindness, as it is said, 'For I desire mercy and not sacrifice' [Hos. 6:6]" (Avot de Rabbi Nathan 4:18).

Based upon the words of this one rabbi, Israel abandoned atonement through the blood and sought it instead through *mitzvot* (good works). As a result, many traditions crept into the observance of Yom Kippur.

However, one Yom Kippur tradition, known as *Kaparot*, still recalls the need for a blood sacrifice. *Kaparot* is observed today only within very orthodox circles and was controversial among early rabbinic authorities as to whether it should be permitted. This ceremony involves the killing of an innocent animal, in particular, a chicken. A chicken is carefully chosen before Yom Kippur and taken to a *shochet* (one trained in the rabbinic laws for slaughtering animals). The observant Jew will grab the chicken with his left hand, place his right hand on its head, and wave the fowl three times overhead while pronouncing, "This is my substitute, my vicarious offering, my atonement. This fowl shall meet death, but I shall enjoy a long, happy life and peace." After reading several selections from Job and the Psalms, the person lays his hand on the head of the bird as a symbol of identification, it is killed as his substitute, and given to the poor for their final meal before the fast.

One may wonder why a chicken is chosen, as opposed to one of the pre-scribed animals for Yom Kippur. The Lord was very clear that sacrifices could be made only in the Temple in Jerusalem (Dt. 12:5-6). After the destruction of the Temple in A.D. 70, it was forbidden to use any animals in a way that might mistakenly continue the sacrificial system. For this rea-son, most Jewish people eat chicken or turkey at Passover instead of a lamb as they did in Bible days. With no Temple in existence today, there are no sacrifices. Yet the observer of *Kaparot* recognizes the weight of God's Word: "'It is the blood that makes atonement for the soul'" (Lev. 17:11). *Kaparot* is the attempt to reconcile the need for atonement through the blood with the absence of the Temple and its sacrificial system. To differ-entiate the *Kaparot* from a sacrifice, a different animal is chosen.

Synagogue Life

The main focus of Yom Kippur today centers upon the synagogue ser-vices. Yom Kippur services usually draw record attendances for the year, and unless one is a member of the synagogue, finding a seat can be diffi-cult.

The synagogue is often decorated in white to symbolize purity and cleansing from transgression. The magnificent, colored tapestry which nor-mally covers the ark for the Torah scroll is replaced with a white one, as is the mantle over the scroll. The reader's table is covered with a white table-cloth, and white flowers decorate the synagogue. Even the worshipers wear white in remembrance of the priests who wore linen in the Temple.

There are five Yom Kippur services in the synagogue, beginning with the *Kol Nidre* service at sundown. The haunting and beautiful melody of the *Kol Nidre* prayer beseeches God to release worshipers from any vows that were made and unknowingly broken during the past year. During the afternoon service, the Book of Jonah is read to focus the people's minds upon repentance and return to God.

An astounding statement is found in the ancient Aramaic *Musaf* prayer for Yom Kippur:

> Our righteous Messiah is departed from us, horror hath seized us, and we have none to justify us. He hath borne the yoke of our iniquities, and our transgressions, and is wounded because of our transgression. He beareth our sins on His shoulder that we may find pardon for our iniquities. We shall be healed by His wounds . . . .

The writer of this ancient prayer correctly understood the words of the Hebrew prophet spoken concerning the Messiah: "Surely He has borne our griefs And carried our sorrows; Yet we esteemed Him stricken, Smitten by God, and afflicted. But He was wounded for our transgressions, He was bruised for our iniquities; The chastisement for our peace was upon Him, And by His stripes we are healed. All we like sheep have gone astray; We have turned, every one, to his own way; And the LORD has laid on Him the iniquity of us all" (Isa. 53:4-6).

 # THE FUTURE FULFILLMENT

Like Israel's other autumn feasts, Yom Kippur prophetically points to Messiah's future work with the nation of Israel. These events will occur in the end of days at Messiah's coming to establish His throne.

 ## Israel's Repentance

The Hebrew prophet, Daniel, outlined a broad timeline of prophetic events for Israel in his "seventy weeks" vision. These prophetic "weeks" (literally, "sevens") measured seven years in length instead of seven days. Many passages substantiate this. Elsewhere, the latter half of the seventieth week is described as $3\frac{1}{2}$ years (Dan. 7:25; 12:7; Rev. 12:14), or 42 months (Rev. 11:2; 13:5), or 1,260 days (Rev. 11:3; 12:6). Seven-year units were very familiar to Israel because of the Sabbatical Year. Together, these seventy "weeks" totaled 490 years (70 x 7 years).

Daniel predicted that there would be sixty-nine seven-year periods (483 years) from "the going forth of the command To restore and build Jerusalem Until Messiah the Prince" (Dan. 9:25). He prophesied that Messiah would be executed ("cut off," Dan. 9:26) after the end of the sixty-ninth week. These sixty-nine weeks of Daniel's vision are now past. They began when the Persian king, Artaxerxes, ordered the rebuilding of Jerusalem (Ezra 7:6-7; 9:9; Neh. 2:5) in the fifth century B.C. and ended just before the Messiah was crucified by the Romans around A.D. 30.

Daniel further predicted that after Messiah's execution there would be an unspecified gap of time before the prophetic clock resumed for the seventieth week (the final seven-year period). During this gap of time, the Gentiles would destroy Jerusalem and the Temple (Dan. 9:26). This was fulfilled when Titus and the Roman army destroyed the Second Temple in A.D. 70. Hosea prophesied that, during this gap, the Messiah would return to Heaven and await the day of Israel's repentance: "I will return again to My place Till they acknowledge their offense. Then they will seek My face; In their affliction they will earnestly seek Me" (Hos. 5:15).

Daniel's seventieth week (the final seven years of this age) is still future. The Bible teaches that it will begin when an evil world ruler arises in the end of days. In Jewish theology, he is known as Armilus. In Christian theology, he is known as Antichrist. In the middle of the seventieth week, he will desecrate the rebuilt Temple with an image of himself and cause the sacrificial system to cease (Dan. 9:27; Mt. 24:15; 2 Th. 2:4). He will persecute the Jewish people, forcing them to flee to the wilderness: "And there shall be a time of trouble, Such as never was since there was a nation, Even to that time" (Dan. 12:1; cf. Jer. 30:7; Rev. 12:6).

But, the Lord will stand up in great wrath to execute His judgment upon the wicked. The Messiah will do battle against His enemies and, at the end of the seventieth week, break the yoke of Gentile oppression from the neck of Israel (Ps. 2:9; Isa. 9:4). Then the messianic throne will be established, "And the LORD shall be King over all the earth" (Zech. 14:9; cf. Ps. 2:8).

When the Messiah comes to establish His throne, Israel will look on Him (Jesus) whom they pierced, and repent (Zech. 12:10). The nation's sin will be dealt with, and the Lord will remember their sin no more (Isa. 43:25; Jer. 31:34). Isaiah prophesied that spiritually the nation would be born in a day (Isa. 66:8; cf. Rom. 11:26). This will be the prophetic fulfillment of Israel's Day of Atonement as the nation comes face to face in repentance with their Messiah at the end of the seventieth week (Dan. 9:24).

The Ark of the Covenant

The Ark of the Covenant is closely associated with Yom Kippur since the high priest only entered the Holy of Holies on Yom Kippur to sprinkle blood upon it. The Ark of the Covenant was seen only on Israel's national day of repentance.

When Solomon's temple was destroyed by the Babylonians in 586 B.C., the Ark of the Covenant was lost. It was never mentioned again in the Hebrew Scriptures and never restored to the Second Temple. Many have speculated that the Ark was hidden to prevent its capture by the Babylonians. This has led to many stories concerning its supposed location. Some believe it was carried to Ethiopia, some believe it was hidden in a cave in Jordan, others believe that it was hidden in a secret place under the Temple Mount, awaiting the rebuilding of the Third Temple. In the final analysis, neither Scripture nor history records the fate of the lost Ark.

However, Scripture teaches that the earthly Temple and its furniture were merely copies of the heavenly temple (Heb. 9:23-24). The real Ark of the Covenant exists in Heaven today. It is very significant, therefore, that at the end of the seventieth week, the heavenly Temple will be opened and the Ark of the Covenant will be seen (Rev. 11:19). It will be Israel's future Yom Kippur when the nation with one heart will say, "Come, and let us return to the LORD" (Hos. 6:1).

 # THE APPLICATION

The Blood Requirement

A blood sacrifice is required by Scripture and is centrally tied to the sin issue. The substitutionary death of an innocent one was required since an atonement (covering) for sin was to be made only through the blood (Lev. 17:11). The New Testament Scriptures remained in agreement: "Without shedding of blood there is no remission" of sins (Heb. 9:22). This concept continued to be strongly taught by the rabbis even a century after Jesus. In the Talmud, the third-century commentary on Jewish belief and practice, it states: "There is no atonement but by blood" (Yoma 5a). The solution to the sin problem was *always* tied to the substitutionary shedding of blood.

I once had the question posed to me by a very observant synagogue officer: "Why did God demand blood, and not some other body fluid, such as sweat or tears?" Scripture teaches that God is a God of absolute justice. He will always do what His pure justice demands. His justice operates within the dual principle that He will judge disobedience (sin) and bless obedience (righteousness). He cannot, and will not, overlook sin. The prophet proclaimed, "You are of purer eyes than to behold evil, And cannot look on wickedness" (Hab. 1:13). The penalty for breaking God's law is death (shedding of blood). His justice demands it, but in

His mercy He made provision for a substitute. That is, for the truly repentant individual, an innocent one could serve as his substitute. Since "There is none who does good, No, not one" (Ps. 14:3), God commanded the sacrificing of lambs, bulls, and goats under the Mosaic Covenant.

The Old Covenant

The prophet Jeremiah foretold of a new covenant which would supersede the Mosaic Covenant. It would be better in that men would be given the power to keep it (i.e., it would be written in their hearts). It would also be better in that it would provide for the *removal* of sins instead of merely *covering* the past year's sins. The Hebrew prophet promised: "Behold, the days are coming, says the LORD, when I will make a new covenant with the house of Israel and with the house of Judah . . . I will put My law in their minds, and write it on their hearts; and I will be their God, and they shall be My people . . . For I will forgive their iniquity, and their sin I will remember no more" (Jer. 31:31-34).

The Old Covenant was only a forerunner, a temporary measure until the fullness of time when God would institute the New Covenant. As the writer of Hebrews said, "For the law made nothing perfect; on the other hand, there is the bringing in of a better hope" (Heb. 7:19). And again, "For the law, having a shadow of the good things to come, and not the very image of the things, can never with these same sacrifices, which they offer continually year by year, make those who approach perfect" (Heb. 10:1).

If the Old Covenant had been sufficient to provide a permanent solution to the sin problem instead of merely a covering, then God would never have promised a second covenant to supersede it (Heb. 8:7).

The relationship of the Old Covenant to the New Covenant can best be illustrated by a credit card. A credit card has no intrinsic value. It is merely plastic. But it is accepted in lieu of cash as if it were a true cash transaction because it is a forerunner, or a shadow, of the true payment which is to follow. The actual payment is made at a later time when the customer pays his credit card bill. Until that time, the credit card *covers* the purchase. In this sense, the sacrifices under the Old Covenant covered sins and foreshadowed the coming day when Jesus would make the true payment upon the Cross. Because the debt has been paid and salvation purchased, there is no need for the credit card (sacrificial system) today. He paid not only all past debts, but all future ones as well. He was the once-for-all payment for sin.

The New Covenant

True Forgiveness

The New Covenant is far superior to the Old Covenant in that it affords true forgiveness and cleansing from sin. There is no covering (atonement) for sin under the New Covenant. There is no need for one. The sin question was settled at Calvary. The Messiah was not our atonement — He did away with our atonement. Therefore, to say that we have an atonement today is highly inaccurate and is never taught in the New Testament. The word *atonement* occurs only once in the New Testament (Romans 5:11) and is a translation of the Greek word which is elsewhere translated *reconciliation*.

The Old Covenant was a *shadow* of things to come. The New Covenant is the *substance*.

Under the Old Covenant, the payment for sin was *anticipated*. Under the New Covenant, it is *realized*.

Under the Old Covenant, the sacrifices were *provisional* and *recurring*. Under the New Covenant, the sacrifice through Jesus' death is *eternal* and *totally sufficient* (Heb. 7:27; 9:12, 25-28).

Under the Old Covenant, men's lambs could only *cover* sin (Heb. 10:4), but under the New Covenant, God's Lamb is able to *take away* sin (Jn. 1:29).

True Security

The New Covenant is also superior in its security and assurance of salvation. The moment one places his trust in the Messiah's sacrifice upon the Cross, the sin question is settled FOREVER. There is no more need for continual sacrifices (Heb. 9:11-14, 24-28; 10:11-20). He did it all!

It should bring great comfort to every believer today to know that His sacrifice was not only perfect and accepted by God, but it was also sufficient, once and for all. There can be no greater security than this.

We do not have to wonder every year whether our names are written in the Book of Life. The Bible assures us that we can know that we have life — not for just another year, but for eternity (1 Jn. 5:13).

 # CONCLUSION

Year after year, the sound of the ram's horn calls Israel to repentance, but there is no atonement in Judaism today. There is no blood sacrifice, no temple, no priesthood, and no adherence to the Levitical regulations.

Within the Jewish breast, a yearning exists for true forgiveness before God. But it will never be found through the traditions of men, such as doing *mitzvot* ("good deeds") or transferring one's guilt to a substitute fowl. It can come only through accepting the infinite sacrifice of Jesus, the Lamb of God.

The Hebrew Scriptures tell us that God provided the Messiah as His "offering for sin" (Isa. 53:10). His is the only sacrifice for sin today. If His sacrifice is rejected, only one tragic alternative remains: men and women must suffer the penalty for their own sin. This penalty is death and eternal separation from God (Isa. 59:2; Rom. 6:23). But to those who have put their trust in Him, he says, "Their sin I will remember no more" (Jer. 31:34).

Have you put your trust in the Lamb of God to take away your sins, or are you still following the traditions of men?

SUKKOT

סוכות

"Speak to the children of Israel, saying: 'The fifteenth day of this seventh month shall be the Feast of Tabernacles for seven days to the LORD'" (Lev. 23:34).

Sukkot –
The Feast of Tabernacles

Kevin L. Howard

The seventh and final feast given to Israel by the Lord is known as *Sukkot* or "The Feast of Tabernacles." It is the most joyful and festive of all Israel's feasts. It is also the most prominent feast, mentioned more often in Scripture than any of the other feasts. This feast also served as the historical backdrop for the important teaching of the Messiah in John, chapters 7-9.

THE BIBLICAL OBSERVANCE

The Meaning of Sukkot

The Feast of Tabernacles is known by at least two names in Scripture. Most often it is referred to as *Sukkot*, or "Tabernacles." The English word "tabernacle" is from the Latin *tabernaculum* meaning "booth" or "hut." It acquired this name from the biblical requirement for all Israelites to dwell in tabernacles or temporary shelters during the holiday. It was to be an annual reminder of God's provision during the forty-year wilderness sojourn when Israel had lived in similar shelters. This final feast of the year is also known in Scripture as "the Feast of Ingathering" (Ex. 23:16; 34:22), for it was observed after all crops had been harvested and gathered.

The feast was celebrated with great joy. The joy was twofold, for it commemorated God's *past* goodness and provision during their wilderness sojourn, and it commemorated God's *present* goodness and provision with the completion of the harvest.

The Time of Sukkot

Tabernacles falls in the autumn of the year. On the Hebrew calendar it occurs on the 15th day of Tishri, the seventh month (usually late September to mid-October), only five days after the solemn Day of Atonement.

The Feast of Tabernacles lasts for seven days. The first day and the day after Tabernacles (the eighth day, known as *Shemini Atzeret*) are considered sacred assemblies, or sabbaths (Lev. 23:36, 39). As such, no work of any kind is permitted on these days.

The Record of Sukkot

Three portions of Scripture outline the biblical observance of the Feast of Tabernacles. The people were to live in booths and rejoice before the Lord with branches (Lev. 23:33-43). There were to be many daily, sacrificial offerings (Num. 29:12-39). In a sabbatical year, the Law was to be publicly read during Tabernacles (Dt. 31:10-13).

The Importance of Sukkot

Because of the joy associated with the Feast of Tabernacles, it became the most prominent of Israel's holidays. It was referred to simply as "the holiday" by the ancient rabbis.

The importance of the Feast of Tabernacles is also seen in its inclusion as one of the three pilgrim feasts. Three times during the year, all Jewish males were required to appear before the Lord in the Temple (the Feast of Unleavened Bread, the Feast of Weeks, and the Feast of Tabernacles — Ex. 23:17; 34:22-23; Dt. 16:16). These were known as the pilgrim feasts because of the required pilgrimage to Jerusalem. During the Feast of Tabernacles, the people brought their tithes and offerings to the Temple, for they were not to "appear before the LORD empty-handed" (Dt. 16:16).

Further importance is seen in the great number of required sacrifices during the feast week. Each day one goat, fourteen lambs, two rams, and a number of bullocks (thirteen on the first day, decreasing by one each day) were offered in the Temple. Each of the sacrifices was offered with its appropriate meal offerings (flour and oil) and drink offerings (wine). All twenty-four divisions of priests shared in the sacrificial duties during the week.

In the days of the Temple, the Feast of Tabernacles was viewed with great awe, for it was during the Feast of Tabernacles that Solomon dedicated the newly built Temple to the Lord. At that ancient observance of Tabernacles (2 Chr. 5:3), the Shekinah glory of the Lord descended from Heaven to light the fire on the altar **e** and fill the Holy of Holies **g** (1 Ki. 8; 2 Chr. 7:1-10).

The Prayer of Sukkot

The Feast of Tabernacles occurs at Israel's change of seasons and marks the beginning of the winter rainy season. One may be surprised to learn that Jerusalem receives as much precipitation each year as London, England (twenty inches). The major difference is that Jerusalem's rainfall occurs between November and March. These refreshing rains bring necessary moisture for working the soil and the sprouting of new crops. If for some reason the weather patterns are such that several weeks of rainfall are missed, a dire water shortage can quickly develop for the coming year's crops. Because the Feast of Tabernacles is observed at this important juncture when the anticipation of rain is at its highest, the two have become inseparably connected. Even today, the prayers for rain remain an important part of Tabernacles' observance.

The Service of Sukkot

In the days of the Temple, Jewish pilgrims flocked to Jerusalem for the Feast of Tabernacles. They came from every village within the nation and from many foreign countries, most often in large caravans for protection. It was a joyous trip with much singing and laughing along the way.

Upon arrival in Jerusalem, the pilgrims focused their energies upon building booths for the feast. By the afternoon of Tishri 14, thousands upon thousands of leafy booths lined the streets and dotted the surrounding fields and hills. All were carefully located within a Sabbath day's journey (a little more than a half mile) of the Temple.

At sundown, the blast of the shofar (ram's horn) from the Temple announced the arrival of the holiday. A sense of increased excitement fell over the city as darkness came. Myriads of twinkling campfires studded the surrounding countryside like an intricate lacework of tiny amber jewels. Well into the night, muffled laughter and cheery conversations could be heard drifting over the night breezes.

The Water-Libation Ceremony

During the Feast of Tabernacles, the intense anticipation of rain came to be reflected in the Temple services. Each morning of Tabernacles, a water libation (sacrificial pouring out of a liquid) was offered to the Lord as a visual prayer for rain.

Shortly after dawn each morning, while the many sacrifices were being prepared, the high priest was accompanied by a joyous procession of music and worshipers down to the Pool of Siloam. The high priest carried a golden pitcher capable of holding a little more than a quart of water. He carefully dipped the pitcher into the pool and brought it back to the Temple Mount.

At the same time, another procession went down to a nearby location south of Jerusalem known as Motza where willows of the brook grew in great abundance. There they gathered the long, thin willows and brought them back to the Temple. At the Temple, the willows were placed on the sides of the altar so that their tops formed a canopy of drooping branches over the altar.

Meanwhile, the high priest with the water from the Pool of Siloam had reached the southern gate of the Temple. It was known as the Water Gate **ⓗ** because of this ceremony. As he entered, three blasts of the silver trumpets sounded from the Temple, and the priests with one voice repeated the words of Isaiah, "Therefore with joy you will draw water From the wells of salvation" (Isa. 12:3).

The high priest slowly proceeded to the great stone altar **ⓔ** in the Inner Court of the Temple and ascended the right side of the ramp. At the peak, he turned to the left where there were two silver basins which drained to the base of the altar. One was reserved for the regular drink offerings (libations of wine) and one for the water libations during this feast.

As the high priest raised the golden pitcher to pour out the water offering, the people shouted, "Raise your hand!" In response, the high priest lifted his hand higher and poured, allowing the people to verify his action. This tradition arose around 95 B.C. in response to an uprising in the days of Alexander Jannaeus, the king-priest grandson of Simon the Maccabee. The Maccabees were a family of priests led by their father, Mattathias, who in 165 B.C. were instrumental in overthrowing Greco-Syrian rule of Israel (see Chapter 12). However, their descendants became a kingly line, wrongfully merging the offices of king and priest. According to Scripture, Israel's kings were to be from the tribe of Judah and lineage of David, and her priests from the tribe of Levi and lineage of Aaron. As a result, Alexander Jannaeus was hated by many of his Jewish brethren. As a Sadducee, he viewed the water pouring with contempt because it was not commanded in the Law of Moses but was a tradition. So instead of pouring the water into the basin, he poured it out upon the ground. The worshipers rioted, pelting him with the citron fruits from their branches, and sought to kill him. In a great rage, Alexander Jannaeus called the foreign mercenary troops of his standing army to quell the riot. When the violent insurrection was finally subdued, six thousand people lay dead, and a horn was broken from the holy altar. Thereafter, the pouring ceremony was always closely scrutinized.

As the high priest poured out the water libation before the Lord, a drink offering of wine was simultaneously poured into the other basin. Three blasts of the silver trumpets immediately followed the pouring and signaled the start of the Temple music. The people listened as a choir of Levites sang the *Hallel* (i.e., the praise Psalms, 113-118).

At the proper time, the congregation waved their palm branches toward the altar and joined in singing: "Save now, I pray, O LORD; O LORD, I pray, send now prosperity" (Ps. 118:25). At the same time the priests, with palm branches in hand, marched once around the altar.

Psalm 118 was viewed as a messianic psalm and as such gave the feast a messianic emphasis. This is why Jesus was greeted by the crowds shouting *Hosanna* (Hebrew for "Save now" in Ps. 118:25) and waving palm branches on His triumphal entry into Jerusalem (Mt. 21:8-9; Lk. 19:38; Jn. 12:13). They viewed Him as the Messiah King, come to deliver ("save now") Israel in fulfillment of Psalm 118. They hailed Him with the messianic imagery of palm branches from the Feast of Tabernacles. This same imagery is in view in Revelation 7:9-10 where redeemed saints worship, with palm branches in hand, around the throne of God and the Lamb.

This custom of carrying branches and singing psalms during the Feast of Tabernacles is of ancient origin. It dates back at least to the time of the Maccabees, some 165 years before Christ (cf. 2 Macc. 10:6-7).

The water-drawing ceremony is also from antiquity. Although debate exists as to whether Isaiah alluded to the water-drawing ceremony (Isa. 12:3) or the ceremony was derived from the words of Isaiah, it is known that the ceremony was in use at least 100 years before the time of Jesus.

The Temple-Lighting Ceremony

The *celebration* of the water pouring (as opposed to the *ceremony*) was observed during the evenings of the feast by an impressive light ceremony in the Temple. It was known as the *Simchat Bet Hasho'ayva* ("the Rejoicing of the House of [Water] Drawing").

As the second evening of Tabernacles approached, the people crowded into the vast outer court of the Temple known as the Court of the Women. ❶ On this occasion a barrier was raised to divide the men from the women. In the center of the court stood four towering menorahs (lampstands), each with four branches of oil lamps. Their wicks were manufactured from the worn-out linen garments of the priests. Each menorah had four long ladders leading up to the lamps which were periodically refilled by young priests carrying large pitchers of olive oil.

The Feast of Tabernacles began in the middle of the lunar month when the harvest moon was full and the autumn sky clear. The outline of the surrounding Judean hills was clearly visible in the soft moonlight. Against this backdrop, the light of the Temple celebration was breathtaking. All night long, elders of the Sanhedrin performed impressive torch dances, while the steady yellow flames of the menorah oil lamps flooded the Temple and the streets of Jerusalem with brilliant light.

Soon after the celebration was underway, a group of Levites gathered in the Inner Court in what was known as the Court of the Israelites. ❹ Once formed, the group of Levites moved through the Nicanor Gate ❶ to stand at the top of the fifteen steps leading down to the Court of the Women. The sound of Temple flutes, trumpets, harps, and other stringed instruments swelled as the Levites sang the fifteen Psalms of Degrees (Psalms 120-134). With each new psalm they descended to the next step.

This celebration was repeated every night from the second night until the final night as a prelude to the water drawing in the morning. Nothing in ancient Israel compared to this light celebration. It was so spectacular that the ancient rabbis said: "He that hath not beheld the joy of the drawing of water [the *Simchat Bet Hasho'ayva* celebration] hath never seen joy in his life" (Sukkah 5:1).

The light celebration was reminiscent of the descent of the Shekinah glory in Solomon's day and looked forward to the return of the Shekinah in the days of the Messiah (Ezek. 43:1-6).

John recorded that it was the day after the Feast of Tabernacles (the eighth day), which was considered a sabbath, when Jesus returned from the Mount of Olives to teach in the Temple (Jn. 8:2; cf. 7:2, 37). As the Pharisees came to entrap Him, Jesus proclaimed, "I am the light of the world. He who follows Me shall not walk in darkness, but have the light of life" (Jn. 8:12). The Pharisees did not question the meaning of His statement. They knew that it was a messianic claim, for they immediately called Him a liar. They were familiar with the many titles in Scripture which ascribe *light* to the Messiah. He is called the "Star out of Jacob," the "light of Israel," the "light of the nations [Gentiles]," a "refiner's fire," a "burning lamp," and the "Sun of righteousness."

Later that day, the Messiah reinforced this same truth when He healed the blind man. As He did so, He repeated, "As long as I am in the world, I am the light of the world" (Jn. 9:5). The Pharisees were again angered at Jesus. The issue continued to be His messiahship (Jn. 9:22). This time, however, they chose to find fault in that He had healed the blind man on the eighth day, which was considered a sabbath by Scripture (Jn. 9:14). Although there were no Mosaic laws against the act of healing on the Sabbath, the traditions of the Pharisees classified it as work and therefore forbade it.

More than just a messianic claim, Jesus' claim to be the "light of the world" carried a reference to the Temple light celebration. The celebration was still vivid in their minds. They had just celebrated it six nights in a row. The light that He offered (i.e., salvation, Isa. 49:6) would light not just the Temple, it would light the whole world. He himself was the source.

The Hoshana-Rabbah Ceremony

On the seventh and final day of the Feast of Tabernacles, the Temple services reached a climax. The anticipation of rain was at its annual high. Jewish tradition held that it was on this day that God declared whether there would be rain for the coming year's crops. Consequently, on this final day of the feast, the Temple water-pouring ritual took on great importance. Water was the foremost thought on everyone's mind.

On the other six days of the feast, the silver trumpets gave *three* blasts. On this day, the trumpets gave *three sets of seven* blasts. On the other six days of the feast, the priests made but *one* circuit around the altar. On this day, the priests made *seven* circuits. As they marched around the altar, they sang the Hosanna verse (Ps. 118:25) and the people waved palm branches. For these reasons, the day was known as the *Hoshana Rabbah*, or "Great

Hosanna." Thoughts of rain for the coming year and messianic fervor (Ps. 118) were at their highest pitch.

The year was somewhere around A.D. 30. It was Hoshana Rabbah, the last day, the great day of the Feast of Tabernacles. The bright morning sun was almost too warm as the throngs crowded the Temple courts for the Hoshana Rabbah service. As the people intently watched the priests conduct the service, a loud voice rang out from the crowd. The priests glared in consternation, and the people whipped around in great surprise to see who dared interrupt the service. They saw a young Galilean in His early thirties, the one whom many held to be a great rabbi, a prophet, or even the Messiah. He boomed: "If anyone thirsts, let him come to Me and drink. He who believes in Me, as the Scripture has said, out of his heart will flow rivers of living water" (Jn. 7:37-38; cf. Jn. 4:14). In other words, He said: *I am the answer to your prayers. I am the Messiah. I can save you now so that you will never thirst for salvation again.*

The sound of His words echoed through their minds in the moment of electric silence that followed. Then the reaction broke loose. The religious leadership was infuriated, indignant, and extremely threatened. Who did He think He was to interrupt the Temple service, and from where did He get His authority to declare Himself the Messiah? He certainly had not been approved by them nor given their sanction to do this. They viewed it as a serious challenge indeed to their religious authority. "Now some of them wanted to take Him, but no one laid hands on Him" (Jn. 7:44).

A spirited debate broke out among the people. They thought Him neither crazy nor unclear. The authoritative claim of His statement was understood by all. But a great debate arose regarding His identity. Some thought He was claiming to be "the Prophet" (Jn. 7:40) that Moses had predicted would appear within Israel (Dt. 18:15). He was. However, in their theology, they believed the prophet was not the same individual as the Messiah (cf. Jn. 1:19-21). Some believed He was claiming to be the Messiah — and, of a truth, He was. However, still others debated this notion with, "Has not the Scripture said that the Christ [the Messiah] comes from the seed of David and from the town of Bethlehem, where David was?" (Jn. 7:42).

These were ignorant that Jesus was, in reality, a descendant of David, and that His birthplace was Bethlehem. So John recorded, "There was a division among the people because of Him" (Jn. 7:43).

In the wake of these disturbing events, the religious leadership called an emergency security meeting. It was a meeting of the chief priests, those twenty-four priests who were head over the twenty-four divisions of the priesthood (1 Chr. 24:1-19). They were aristocratic Sadducees who controlled the *Temple* worship. Also present were the Pharisees. They were the perpetuators of the oral, extrabiblical traditions within Israel. They controlled the *synagogue* worship. These two groups, usually at great odds over theology and engaged in religious power struggles, were united in their hatred of Jesus.

They summoned the officers to give an account as to why they had not arrested Jesus. The officers were Levites who patrolled the Temple compound and enforced Temple law. They were the security force, the Temple guard, whose responsibility it would have been to arrest Jesus for interrupting the service. A few days earlier, the officers had been commanded to arrest Jesus (Jn. 7:14, 30-32), but now they had missed the perfect occasion to do so. The officers, too, had been stunned by His statement, for they answered in their defense, "No man ever spoke like this Man!" (Jn. 7:46). After being rebuked in great rage, the officers were sent away.

■ ■■■■■■■ THE MODERN OBSERVANCE

The Tabernacles

The primary symbol of the Feast of Tabernacles is the *sukkah* or tabernacle. It recalls Israel's hastily built housing in the wilderness. As soon as Yom Kippur is past, booths are constructed in yards and patios of Jewish homes. The booths are made with no fewer than three walls covered with intertwined branches. The roofs are thatched so that there is more shade than sunlight during the day, but sparsely enough to allow the stars to be seen at night. Inside they are decorated with colorful harvest fruits and vegetables. During the Feast of Tabernacles, Jewish families eat their meals in the booths, and the very observant even sleep in them.

The Branches

" 'And you shall take for yourselves on the first day the fruit of beautiful trees, branches of palm trees, the boughs of leafy trees, and willows of the brook; and you shall rejoice before the LORD your God for seven days' " (Lev. 23:40).

A controversy arose between the Sadducees and Pharisees as to the interpretation of this passage. The Sadducees believed that this referred to the material to be used in building the booths. The Pharisees believed it referred to the branches to be carried in the hands of joyful worshipers. A compromise was struck, and both practices were observed.

Since the Scripture mentions four types of trees, four types are literally used to fulfill this command. They are referred to as the "four species." The *etrog*, a tree which produces small lemon-like fruit, is interpreted by Jewish authorities to be the "beautiful trees." The *lulav*, or long branch of a date palm, is held to be the "palm trees." The *hadas*, or myrtle tree, with its tiny leaves, is believed to be the "leafy trees." Usually three myrtle branches are held in the hand. The *arava*, or willow tree, is used in fulfillment of the "willows of the brook." Usually two willow branches are held since the Scripture mentions them in the plural. The *etrog*, or citrus branch, is held in the left hand, and the other three types of branches are bound together and held in the right hand. As in the ancient Temple services, the branches are held while the Hosanna verse (Ps. 118:25) is chanted.

The Synagogue

As a preservation of the ancient Temple ceremony, all congregants circle the synagogue while singing Psalm 118. The Torah scroll on the center platform of the synagogue, instead of the ancient altar, is the object of the procession today.

After the cessation of the Temple services, the Feast of Tabernacles became more closely tied to Yom Kippur which occurs only five days earlier on the Hebrew calendar. Hoshana Rabbah, the last day of the feast, came to be viewed as the last day on which the judgments meted out by God on Yom Kippur could be reversed. On this day, willow branches are ceremonially beaten on the synagogue pews to remove the leaves, symbolizing repentance and removal of sins.

The Rejoicing

Even though the Temple water-drawing ceremony and light celebration do not exist today, the concept of rejoicing is still connected with the Feast of Tabernacles. In the Middle Ages, a new holiday arose known as *Simchat Torah* ("the Rejoicing of the Law"). It occurs on the ninth day (or the eighth day in Israel) from the start of the Feast of Tabernacles. This post-biblical holiday preserves the traditions of rejoicing and the reading of the Law of Moses during Tabernacles (Dt. 31:10-13). During the year, the entire Law (the Five Books of Moses) is read, a portion at a time, each Sabbath. On Simchat Torah, the annual cycle of reading the Law begins again. The last chapter of Deuteronomy and the first chapter of Genesis are read as the cycle begins anew. Everyone in the synagogue receives an *aliyah* (an opportunity to read the Scriptures from the pulpit). Afterward the congregation marches around the synagogue with great rejoicing as the uplifted Torah scroll leads the procession.

 # THE FUTURE FULFILLMENT

The Ingathering

The Bible often speaks of the final judgment as a harvest (Hos. 6:11; Joel 3:13; Mt. 13:39; Rev. 14:15). It is a future *Day of Ingathering* when God gathers His people unto Himself and burns the wicked like the chaff and stubble (Mal. 4:1-2). So it is not surprising that the Feast of Tabernacles is tied to Israel's future as well as her past.

When the Messiah sets up His millennial Kingdom, He will gather the remnant of Israel back to her land. Isaiah described this event as the harvesting of olives. Tree branches are beaten with rods and the olive berries gathered once they fall to the ground. "And it shall come to pass in that day That the LORD will thresh, From the channel of the River to the Brook of Egypt; And you will be gathered one by one, O you children of Israel. So it shall be in that day: The great trumpet will be blown; They will come, who are about to perish in the land of Assyria, And they who are outcasts in the land of Egypt, And shall worship the LORD in the holy mount at Jerusalem" (Isa. 27:12-13; cf. Isa. 11:11-12; Jer. 23:7-8).

The righteous among the Gentiles, too, will be gathered to the Lord. In that day, the Gentiles will pray in Jerusalem. Zechariah prophesied: "And it shall come to pass that everyone who is left of all the nations which came against Jerusalem shall go up from year to year to worship the King, the LORD of hosts, and to keep the Feast of Tabernacles. And it shall be that whichever of the families of the earth do not come up to Jerusalem to worship the King, the LORD of hosts, on them there will be no rain" (Zech. 14:16-17).

The Gentile nations that refuse to keep the Feast of Tabernacles in the millennial Kingdom will receive no rain upon their lands. This passage provided the biblical basis for the tradition of praying for rain during the Feast of Tabernacles.

The Tabernacle

The Lord will not only gather His people, but He will *tabernacle* in their midst during the coming messianic Kingdom: "My tabernacle also shall be with them; indeed, I will be their God, and they shall be My people. The nations also will know that I, the LORD, sanctify Israel, when My sanctuary is in their midst forevermore" (Ezek. 37:27-28; cf. Rev. 21:3).

The sign of God's presence, the Shekinah glory, will be seen in Zion again (Isa. 60:1, 19; Zech. 2:5). It will appear as a shining fire over the whole of Mount Zion. It will be like a *tabernacle*, providing protection and refuge for the nation after centuries of persecution and the time of Jacob's sore trouble. Isaiah prophesied: "Then the LORD will create above every dwelling place of Mount Zion, and above her assemblies, a cloud and smoke by day and the shining of a flaming fire by night. For over all the glory there will be a covering. And there will be a *tabernacle* for shade in the daytime from the heat, for a place of refuge, and for a shelter from storm and rain" (Isa. 4:5-6).

 THE APPLICATION

Light

When the Messiah spoke of Himself as the light of the world, He referred to the salvation and forgiveness of sins that He offered to all those who put their trust in Him. As it was spoken by the Lord through the prophet Isaiah, "'I will also give You as a light to the Gentiles, That You should be My salvation to the ends of the earth'" (Isa. 49:6). He offers that light to men today: "He who follows Me shall not walk in darkness, but have the light of life" (Jn. 8:12). Have you experienced the life-changing light of the Messiah, or are you still walking in darkness?

Water

There are three types of water sources in the land of Israel. Huge, rock-hewn collection tanks, known as cisterns, are used to collect rainwater during the rainy months. Massive cisterns, capable of holding millions of gallons of water, still exist today at the Masada stronghold. However, cisterns are the least desirable and valuable water source in Israel — they can easily become contaminated or stagnant and are not replenishable until the next rainy season. Wells are a more valuable water source. They provide fresh, replenished water, but even they can dry up during a drought. The most valued water source in Israel are brooks and rivers which are fed by springs (such as those at Ein Gedi). These were known in the Bible as "living waters" or, in other words, waters with movement.

The Lord used this truth to illustrate Israel's rebellion and idolatry: "For My people have committed two evils: They have forsaken Me, the fountain of living waters, And hewn themselves cisterns – broken cisterns that can hold no water" (Jer. 2:13).

When Jesus addressed the people in the Temple on the last day of the feast, He alluded to the same fact. He said, "He who believes in Me, as the Scripture has said, out of his heart will flow *rivers of living water*" (Jn. 7:38). This was the purest water, the most valued water, water that would never dry up.

Ancient Jewish theology connected the water-drawing ceremony with the Holy Spirit. "Why do they call it 'the house of drawing'? Because there they draw the Holy Spirit" (Gen. Rab. 70:1). And again, "Why is the name of it called, the drawing out of water? Because of the pouring out of the Holy Spirit according to what is said: 'With joy shall ye draw water out of the wells of salvation'" (Ruth Rab. 4:7). They believed that the Holy Spirit came upon them and manifested Himself through great joy.

Jesus' reference to water was used with the exact same connection: "But this He spoke concerning the Spirit, whom those believing in Him would receive" (Jn. 7:39).

The outpouring of the Holy Spirit in relation to salvation was a much-repeated theme of the Old Testament prophets (Isa. 32:15; 59:21; Ezek. 11:19; 36:27; 37:14; 39:29; Joel 2:28-29). The Lord said through Isaiah, "For I will pour *water* on him who is thirsty, And floods on the dry ground; I will pour *My Spirit* on your descendants" (Isa. 44:3).

The Hebrew prophet Zechariah prophesied of a future, glorious day when Israel as a nation will look upon the pierced Messiah and repent of her rejection of Him. God's Spirit will be poured out upon them and they will enter into the New Covenant. "And I will *pour* on the house of David and on the inhabitants of Jerusalem *the Spirit* of grace and supplication; then they will look on Me whom they pierced. Yes, they will mourn for Him as one mourns for his only son, and grieve for Him as one grieves for a firstborn" (Zech. 12:10).

Do you thirst today to have a living relationship with the Creator and God of the Universe and to know that you have eternal life? Jesus said, "If anyone thirsts, let him come to Me and drink" (Jn. 7:37). There is only one water that will quench the spiritual thirst of man. It is the living water offered by the Lord.

תשעה באב

"Should I weep in the fifth month and fast as I have done for so many years?" (Zech. 7:3).

Tisha B'Av – The Fast of the Fifth Month

Kevin L. Howard

During the heat of midsummer, observant Jews busy themselves making preparations as if mourning the death of a loved one. In reality, these preparations are for *Tisha B'Av*. This little-known fast is less understood than Israel's other holy days, but is of considerable importance.

THE HISTORICAL BACKGROUND

The Meaning of Tisha B'Av

Tisha B'Av commemorates what are generally acknowledged to be the two most tragic events of Jewish history. It was on this day that the Babylonians destroyed Solomon's Temple in 586 B.C., and on this day in A.D. 70 that the Romans leveled the Second Temple with fire. Tisha B'Av is therefore set aside as a very somber fast on the Jewish calendar.

Tisha B'Av literally means "the ninth of Av," indicating the date on which this fast is observed. If the ninth happens to be a Sabbath, the fast is postoned until the tenth. Av is the fifth month of the biblical calendar and generally corresponds with July or August on the secular calendar.

The Record of Tisha B'Av

The destruction of Solomon's Temple was not a solitary, isolated event. Its final destiny was determined by a succession of sad steps along the way. A heavy chain of grievous sin and rebellion had been forged around the neck of the Jewish nation for more than a century, interrupted only by the righteous reign of King Josiah. Like mighty links in a long chain, wicked king after wicked king spurned the divine call for repentance and drew the senseless nation ever closer toward the fury of the impending judgment.

In 608 B.C., Jehoiakim became king of Judah. He relentlessly continued to do "evil in the sight of the LORD, according to all that his fathers had done" (2 Ki. 23:37). Therefore, three years later, the Lord caused Jerusalem to fall into the hands of Nebuchadnezzar, the mighty king of Babylon. Nebuchadnezzar subjected Judah to heavy taxes as a vassal state and carried away many of the nobility to Babylon, including Daniel and his three friends (Dan. 1:1-3, 6).

But Jehoiakim defiantly refused to repent of his wickedness. He continually despised the word of the Lord and sought to do away with the prophet Jeremiah. When this failed, he barred Jeremiah (who was a priest) from the Temple to silence his faithful and uncompromising preaching. The Lord then commanded Jeremiah to dictate his prophecies to his scribe Baruch to be read in the Temple. This incensed the wicked king. Jehoiakim confiscated the sacred scroll, cut it into pieces, and burned the words of the Lord to warm his winter palace (Jer. 36). But the word of the Lord was not thwarted. A few years later, Jehoiakim rebelled against Babylon and was subsequently carried off in chains and humiliation along with many of the golden vessels from the Temple.

His son Jehoiachin reigned for a brief three months in 597 B.C. before he was deposed by Nebuchadnezzar. Jehoiachin was exiled to Babylon along with "all Jerusalem: all the captains and all the mighty men of valor, ten thousand captives, and all the craftsmen and smiths. None remained except the poorest people of the land" (2 Ki. 24:14). The prophet Ezekiel was also carried away during this second deportation and prophesied for the remainder of his days in Babylon as a contemporary of Daniel.

In his place, Nebuchadnezzar appointed Zedekiah, the uncle of Jehoiachin, as the new puppet-king of Judah. Yet, even with abundant evidence of divine judgment on every hand, Zedekiah continued to do "evil in the sight of the LORD his God, and did not humble himself . . . . Moreover all the leaders of the priests and the people transgressed more and more, according to all the abominations of the nations . . . . But they mocked the messengers of God, despised His words, and scoffed at His prophets, until the wrath of the LORD arose against His people, till there was no remedy" (2 Chr. 36:12, 14, 16).

The die was finally cast. Divine judgment was no longer delayed. In the ninth year of Zedekiah's reign, Nebuchadnezzar came up against Jerusalem to crush a new rebellion. Jerusalem fell in 586 B.C. after a blistering year-and-a-half siege. It was chronicled in the history of the Jewish kings

(2 Ki. 25:3-4) that the walls of Jerusalem were breached by the Babylonians on the ninth day of Tammuz (the fourth month). Zedekiah was captured and brutally punished. His last sight was the scene of his sons being executed before him. His eyes were then put out, and he was carried away to die in Babylon.

A few weeks later, after all the executions and deportations were sorted out, the captain of the Babylonian army finished his directive. Beginning on the seventh of Av and continuing through the tenth of Av, he set his army on a burning rampage. Every section of Jerusalem's magnificent walls was battered and toppled to the ground. For four days the Babylonians torched the palaces of the royal family and the mansions of the rich. They stripped the breathtaking Temple of all its gold, silver, and brass. Finally, they reduced to ashes the house which the Lord had chosen to call His own. And so for seventy years, the Jewish people were to weep by the rivers of Babylon, captives in a strange land, crying, "If I forget you, O Jerusalem, Let my right hand forget its skill!" (Ps. 137:5).

Jeremiah was an eyewitness to that ultimate tragedy of his people. He not only recorded the events (Jeremiah 52), but his writings and prayers were forever affected by the realities of that terrifying judgment. The horror and pain of those events so weighed upon him that he is known to us today as "the weeping prophet."

And so it was that the ninth of Av became a national day of grieving and fasting over the destruction of the Temple. Seventy years later, Zechariah referred to Tisha B'Av as the fast of the fifth month (Zech. 8:19). He described it as a time of separating oneself through weeping, mourning, and fasting (Zech. 7:3, 5).

But the tragic saga was to continue. Six centuries later, Israel repeated her sin with the same disastrous results. This time she rejected her greatest prophet, the Messiah. On the ninth of Av, A.D. 70, her glorious rebuilt Temple was destroyed by the Romans. Only a small section of the wall surrounding the Temple Mount (known today as the Western Wall) remained standing. The Messiah saw this towering tragedy coming and lamented: "'O Jerusalem, Jerusalem, the one who kills the prophets and stones those who are sent to her! How often I wanted to gather your children together, as a hen gathers her chicks under her wings, but you were not willing! See! Your house is left to you desolate'.... Then Jesus went out and departed from the temple, and His disciples came up to show Him the buildings of the temple. And Jesus said to them, 'Do you not see all these things? Assuredly, I say to you, not one stone shall be left here upon another, that shall not be thrown down'" (Mt. 23:37-38; 24:1-2).

THE MODERN OBSERVANCE

A Time of Calamity

Throughout Jewish history, several other calamities have coincided with Tisha B'Av, serving only to intensify the deep grief for the loss of both temples. In A.D. 135, the Bar Kochba rebellion was violently crushed by the Romans at Betar, ending any hope for Jewish independence for 1,800 years. In A.D. 1290, all Jews were expelled from England on Tisha B'Av for no crime other than being Jewish. On Tisha B'Av A.D. 1492, the Catholic King Ferdinand and Queen Isabella of Spain launched the Inquisition. Hundreds of thousands of Spanish Jews were commanded to convert to Catholicism or be burned at the stake. The nightmare of bloodshed, persecution, and tears which followed uprooted and destroyed one of the largest and most influential Jewish communities of all time. Today, Tisha B'Av has come to be regarded as a symbol of all the tragedies of the Jewish people.

A Time of Mourning

Personal

The observance of Tisha B'Av is marked by many of the Jewish customs for mourning the death of a loved one. The time of grieving begins during the month of Tammuz since this was the month that the invading forces breached the walls of Jerusalem. This time period is known as the *Three Weeks* or *Between the Straits*, taken from the verse, "All her [Judah's] persecutors overtook her *in dire straits*" (Lam. 1:3). During the Three Weeks, no weddings or festive celebrations are held. Observant Jews also do not cut their hair or wear new clothing during this time.

On the first of Av, the mourning escalates. During these final nine days, no wine or meat is eaten because these were traditionally viewed as festive foods. Dairy foods are commonly eaten instead.

The final meal before Tisha B'Av is a mourner's meal. Round-shaped foods like hard-boiled eggs, lentils, rolls, and bagels are normally eaten. That which is round is often thought to be symbolic of eternity with no beginning or ending. These foods are also usually eaten after a Jewish funeral.

Since Tisha B'Av is a major fast day, all food and drink is banned. On this day it is also forbidden to wear shoes, bathe, wear perfume, shave, wash clothes, or exchange greetings. Mirrors are traditionally covered, and mourners sit on the ground or a low stool just as one would do when mourning the loss of a loved one.

Synagogue

The focus on mourning is also carried over to synagogue worship for Tisha B'Av. Synagogue lights are dimmed, and only a few candles are lit to symbolize the great darkness Israel suffered when the Temple was destroyed. The beautifully embroidered curtain over the ark (where the scrolls are kept) is removed, symbolizing the destruction of the great curtain which had hung in the entrance to the Holy of Holies **g**. Worshipers sit on low benches or on the floor and remove their shoes as a sign of mourning. Worshipers sometimes also sprinkle ashes on their heads and on the Torah scrolls.

The mood for the synagogue service is somber. Prayers and Scripture readings are chanted in hushed, melancholy tones. The assigned Scripture reading from the Prophets is Jeremiah 8:13-9:23 where the prophet is overcome by agony and grief at the sin of the people. The entire scroll of Lamentations is also read during the service. Worshipers listen with aching hearts to the intense distress of Jeremiah as he laments the devastation of his people and capital city: "My eyes fail with tears . . . Because of the destruction of the daughter of my people [Jerusalem]" (Lam. 2:11).

Israel

For almost two thousand years, Gentile domination has prevented the Jewish people from praying on the Temple Mount. In 1995, Israel's courts approved Tisha B'Av (the day on which both Temples were destroyed) as the one day of the year that Jews may pray on the Temple Mount. However,

at the time of the writing of this book, the Jewish people still have not been able to exercise that right due to riots and aggression by the Moslems. Moslems, on the other hand, freely pray on Israel's Temple Mount every day of the year. The heartache of this situation is a constant reminder that Israel still awaits her final redemption.

So when will the fast of Tisha B'Av end? Is Israel forever destined to mourn her sin and the loss of her holy Temple? The question is so pressing that the Lord himself answers: "Thus says the LORD of hosts: 'The fast of the fourth month, The fast of the fifth . . . Shall be joy and gladness and cheerful feasts For the house of Judah. Therefore love truth and peace'" (Zech. 8:19).

There is a day coming, perhaps even in our days, when the Lord will turn away His anger and send the Messiah, "And He shall build the temple of the LORD" (Zech. 6:12). All of human history has been awaiting that day. Israel's sins will be remembered no more (Jer. 31:34) and her holy Temple will be restored, far more glorious than can even be imagined. Most importantly, the Lord will reign from that new Temple. "Sing and rejoice, O daughter of Zion! For behold, I am coming and I will dwell in your midst . . . . Rejoice greatly, O daughter of Zion! Shout, O daughter of Jerusalem! Behold, your King is coming to you . . . . And the LORD shall be King over all the earth" (Zech. 2:10; 9:9; 14:9).

In that day there will be no need for fasting. With the Messiah ruling from His holy Temple, Tisha B'Av will become Israel's great day of joy and gladness!

חנוכה

"Now it was the Feast of Dedication in Jerusalem, and it was winter. And Jesus walked in the temple, in Solomon's porch" (Jn. 10:22-23).

Hanukkah —
The Feast of Dedication

Kevin L. Howard

They are called the "Four hundred silent years," the time between the testaments; called "silent" because during that time God gave no new revelation to His people. From Malachi until John the Baptist, the prophetic voice in Israel was silent. There were no prophets, no visions, and no angelic visits. However, prophetic silence did not indicate that God had forgotten His people.

Many significant events in Israel's history occurred during those four centuries — the development of the synagogue, the rise of the Sadducees and Pharisees, and the domination by Rome. Perhaps none were more important than the events that gave occasion to the Jewish holiday of Hanukkah.

 ## THE HISTORICAL BACKGROUND

The Meaning of Hanukkah

Hanukkah is the Hebrew word for "dedication." The holiday is so named because it celebrates the *rededication* of the Temple to the Lord after it was desecrated by the Gentiles. The Hanukkah story preserves the epic struggle and the heroic exploits of one of the greatest Jewish victories of all time — the independence from Greco-Syrian oppression in 165 B.C.

The Time of Hanukkah

Hanukkah is an eight-day feast which occurs near the beginning of winter. On the Hebrew calendar, it is celebrated beginning with the twenty-fifth day of Kislev, the ninth Hebrew month (corresponding roughly to December). The holiday begins only seventy-five days after Yom Kippur, Israel's Day of Atonement.

The Record of Hanukkah

Although Hanukkah as a holiday is not described in Scripture, it still is the most historically documented of all the Jewish holidays. The books of 1 and 2 Maccabees are the earliest historical record of Hanukkah. They are among the fourteen books of the Old Testament Apocrypha, a collection of non-inspired Jewish writings written between 200 B.C. and A.D. 100. Although the overwhelming majority of conservative scholars — both Jewish and Christian, ancient and modern — rightfully reject 1 and 2 Maccabees as part of the Bible, they do remain a valuable historical record.

The Origin of Hanukkah

The Macedonian

The year was 336 B.C., and the winds of change were beginning to blow. Turbulence swept through the ancient world that would forever shape the history of mankind. That year, Darius III came to the mighty Medo-Persian throne which ruled the world. But of greater significance, another king ascended to a throne in the west. He was Alexander, son of Philip II, king of the Greek city-state, Macedonia. Though only twenty years of age, Alexander was nothing short of a brilliant commander. The might and wealth of the Persian empire dwarfed his own, but his sheer military genius enabled him to move with lightning speed against the Persians. In 332 B.C., only some three years later, the armies of Alexander the Great defeated Darius III at Issus.

By age thirty, Alexander had conquered all the then-known world from Europe, to Egypt, to the borders of India. True to his teacher, Aristotle, Alexander unified his empire through the cohesive force of Greek culture and religion known as Hellenism.

The golden age of the Greek empire, like a shooting star, was brief, lasting but a few short years. At age thirty-three, Alexander the Great died an untimely death without an heir, and the rule of his empire was passed to his four generals. They geographically divided the vast Grecian empire into four parts with Seleucus ruling Syria and Eastern Asia Minor, Ptolemy ruling Egypt, Lysimachus ruling Thrace and Western Asia Minor (Turkey), and Cassander ruling Macedonia and Greece.

The Madman

Had it not been for her geographical location, the tiny vassal state of Israel would certainly have gone unnoticed amidst the swirling-wind currents of the ancient world. But such was not the case. Israel was strategically located between Syria and Egypt, the land bridge between the continents of Asia, Africa, and Europe. Control of Israel was key to dominance in the region. With the death of Alexander, Israel again found herself at the center of the maelstrom. For almost two centuries, she was tossed like a leaf in the wind between the expansionistic Seleucid (Syrian) and Ptolemaic (Egyptian) dynasties that sought to dominate the Middle East.

In 171 B.C., Antiochus IV came to the Seleucid throne in Syria. He was a tyrant — cruel, harsh, and savage. He wore his pride like a garment. Believing that he was deity in the flesh, he referred to himself as *Antiochus Theos Epiphanes* ("Antiochus, the visible god"), or just Antiochus Epiphanes. His detractors called him *Epimanes* or "madman." Without warning, Israel found herself exposed to the gale-force winds of his intolerant rule.

Antiochus was anxious to unite his kingdom of many languages, cultures, and religions. These diversities only served to fan the fires of individual nationalism and independence. He desired to "hellenize," or impose Greek language, thought, and religion upon his subjects in an effort to unify his rule through assimilation.

In response, two political factions developed within Israel. The religious in Israel comprised the Orthodox party. They desired rule by the Ptolemies in Egypt since that dynasty did not seek to hellenize its subjects. For Hellenism was far more than just Greek philosophy and ordered society — it was built around the Greek religion. It deified nature, created a pantheon of mythological gods, and promoted widespread immorality in the worship of those gods. The Orthodox party was committed to preserving Judaism and the pure worship of the God of Israel.

Conversely, there were those of the "progressive" Hellenist party. They included many of the aristocracy who had little concern for the faith of their fathers. They saw only the economic and social advantages of appearing enlightened, civilized, and accepted by the advanced nations throughout the world which embraced Hellenism. Therefore, these Hellenists desired Syrian rule along with its imposed Greek culture. This group willingly "forsook" (the Greek word means to "apostatize" or "abandon") the holy covenant (1 Macc. 1:15).

In Jerusalem, Yohanan (Onias III) was high priest and was vehemently opposed to Hellenistic forces within the nation. His brother, Joshua, however, was not of the same conviction. Joshua changed his name to the Greek name of Jason and led the Hellenistic faction. Many in Israel supported him and desired a covenant with the Greeks (1 Macc. 1:11). Seizing the opportunity, Jason offered an enormous bribe to Antiochus Epiphanes to obtain the office of high priest. He also promised to build a temple to the Greek god, Phallus, and a gymnasium (where men performed naked) in Jerusalem, and to enroll the people of Jerusalem as citizens of Antioch, the capital of Syria. Antiochus gladly gave his consent, and Jason became high priest. When Jason had his brother killed by assassins, Israel became a cauldron of internal strife. Never before had an outsider dared to tamper with the divinely instituted high priesthood.

To further intensify the situation, three years later Menelaus, a rabid Hellenist and not even from the high-priestly family, obtained the high priest's office by an even larger bribe. Once in office, he was disappointed to learn that the Temple treasury (from offerings of the people) could not support the payment of his bribe, so he stole the golden vessels from the Temple to pay his bribe to Antiochus.

Meanwhile, the ambitions of Antiochus Epiphanes continued to grow. He aspired to reunify the Grecian empire as in the days of Alexander the Great. In 168 B.C., he warred against Egypt, and victory seemed certain. However, the Roman Senate dispatched Popillius Laenas to prevent Antiochus from taking Egypt. When asked if he wished peace or war with Rome, Antiochus stalled for time. The Roman representative drew a circle in the sand around Antiochus and stated that he must decide before leaving the circle. Consequently, Antiochus was forced to withdraw from Egypt in great humiliation.

On his return to Syria, Antiochus stopped in Jerusalem. Already in a great rage because of Roman interference, he learned that Jason had mounted a rebellion against Menelaus after hearing a rumor of Antiochus' death. Antiochus was incensed by this mockery and challenge to his authority. The continued political intrigue within Israel and deep-seated resistance to Hellenization had run its full course with his patience. And so, suddenly, without warning, Antiochus ordered his general to destroy Jerusalem. The full heat of his wrath and frustration was vented on the Jewish people. Houses were burned, the walls of the city were breached, and tens of thousands were killed or sold into slavery.

But his destruction did not cease. Antiochus turned his attention to the Temple on Mount Zion. Syrian soldiers hacked and smashed the porches and gates. They stripped the Temple of its golden vessels and treasures. On Kislev 15, 168 B.C., Antiochus erected an idol of Zeus, the supreme deity of the Greek pantheon, on the holy altar **ⓔ** in the courtyard. Not surprisingly, it bore the face of Antiochus. On the birthday of Zeus (Kislev/December 25), Antiochus offered a pig on the altar. The pig was the ultimate abomination to the Jewish mind, strictly forbidden by the law of God. Antiochus sprinkled its blood in the Holy of Holies **ⓖ** and poured its broth over the holy scrolls before he cut them to pieces and burned them. The shock! The horror! The nation reeled with severe trauma. The Sanctuary of the Most High had been polluted and profaned. It had been desecrated and defiled. In the words of 1 Maccabees, it was "laid waste like a wilderness" (1 Macc. 1:39) and "trodden down" (1 Macc. 3:45) and, as a result, the nation was left utterly desolate.

The Temple was converted to a shrine to Zeus, and only swine were permitted for sacrifice. A fortress, called the Acra, was erected adjacent to the Temple so that a Syrian garrison could control the shrine.

Furthermore, Antiochus issued an edict forbidding the practice of Judaism on pain of death and enforced it by house searches. If Sabbath was observed, or dietary laws kept, or circumcision performed, or scrolls of the law found, the whole family was put to death. Babies were hung around their mothers' necks and women were thrown from the walls of the cities. The line had been drawn — either assimilate or be annihilated.

The Martyrs

Dark days followed, filled with terror and persecution. The faithful immediately fled to the wilderness or to the Judean hills to live in caves. But they were hunted like animals. During that time of intense suffering, thousands sacrificed their lives to remain true to their God.

Jewish history records several such heroic acts of faithful devotion. Eleazar, ninety years of age and one of the principal scribes (one skilled in the science of hand-copying Scripture), was brought before Antiochus and commanded to eat swine's flesh. He refused to defile himself and break the law of God. So the soldiers asked him to bring his own lawful meat and eat it as if it were the detestable pork. After an eloquent statement of faith he remained unmoved, not willing to deceive the young people with his example. With that, the soldiers beat him mercilessly until he died.

Another account relates the enduring courage of a woman named Hannah and her seven sons. They, too, were arrested and compelled to eat swine's flesh and thereby assent to the pagan sacrifice. One by one the sons were tortured, and when they refused to yield, they were boiled alive in cauldrons. When one son was approached to apostatize or have his tongue and hands cut off, he courageously testified, "These I had from heaven; and for his laws I despise them; and from him I hope to receive them again" (2 Macc. 7:11). Another affirmed before he died, "It is good, being put to death by men, to look for hope from God to be raised up again by him" (2 Macc. 7:14). As the last son was pressed to deliver himself by apostatizing, his mother encouraged him with the resurrection:

> But doubtless the Creator of the world, who formed the generation of man, and found out the beginning of all things, will also of his own mercy give you breath and life again . . . Fear not this tormentor, but, being worthy of thy brethren take thy death, that I may receive thee again in mercy with thy brethren (2 Macc. 7:23, 29).

Finally, the mother was put to death. All steadfastly refused deliverance in hope of the resurrection.

Mattathias

The untold pain of the Jewish nation continued. Syrian detachments were dispatched throughout the nation to enforce the diabolical plan of Antiochus. One such detachment came to the tiny village of Modin (about 17 miles northwest of Jerusalem). There they built a pagan altar to Zeus. The townspeople were assembled, and an aged priest named Mattathias was singled out of the crowd. He was ordered to offer a sacrificial pig to the Greek gods in honor of Antiochus.

Mattathias' head of gray hair was visible testimony to the respect that he carried with the people. He was the great-grandson of Hasmon, a descendant of Jehoiarib of the first division of priests. He was also the father of five sons — John, Simon, Judah, Eleazar, and Jonathan. But now all eyes were upon him. What would he do?

"Never," he replied with defiance. At that moment an apostate priest approached the altar and requested permission to offer the pig. The onlookers knew what would follow. After the sacrifice, they would all be forced to eat its flesh in identification with the offering.

Indignation stirred in the heart of Mattathias and erupted into violence. He ripped the sword from the hand of the Syrian officer and killed him. Rushing forward, he ran the sword through the body of the apostate Jew and left him lying on the altar. His five sons simultaneously engaged and slew the remaining soldiers in the commotion. Quickly, they pulled down the altar. Knowing that severe retribution would be taken, they and the faithful of the city fled to the hills of Judea, leaving all possessions behind.

And so the revolt began — an uprising against the enemies of the one true God.

The Maccabees

Each day the faithful band grew as the word of the rebellion spread. They engaged in guerrilla warfare, attacking Syrian outposts, destroying pagan altars, and chastising apostate sympathizers. Within the year, the aged Mattathias grew sick and died. On his deathbed, leadership was passed to his son Judah.

Judah was a wise choice, a military genius in his own right. He was called *the Maccabee*, believed to be from the Hebrew word *makkevet* meaning "hammer." It spoke of the sheer might of his military prowess.

For three years the revolt raged. Hiding in caves and lying in ambush, the Maccabees gradually frustrated and wore down the Syrian occupation. Finally the freedom fighters met the enemy in open battle. They secured stunning victories at Beth-horon and Emmaus, opening the road to Jerusalem.

The Mending of the Altar

The forces of Judah were hardly prepared for what they were to encounter in Jerusalem. The gates of the Temple were burned, weeds grew waist-high in its courtyards, and above it all loomed the hideous Zeus-idol with the face of Antiochus. They ripped their clothes and threw handfuls of dust on their heads as they wept. Oh, how desolate the nation had been made!

The liberators immediately began to cleanse the Sanctuary. They removed the defilement and the Greek idol. Because of the pollution to the altar, they pulled down its stones and stored them "until there should come a prophet to give an answer concerning them" (1 Macc. 4:44-46). They rebuilt the holy altar and on Kislev 25, 165 B.C., exactly three years to the day from its defilement, they rededicated the altar to the Lord.

The Miracle

According to Jewish tradition in the Talmud (Shabbat 21b), the Maccabees found only one small cruse of unpolluted oil in the Temple which still bore the unbroken seal of the high priest. It was but one day's supply for the golden lampstand. Miraculously, it burned for eight days until a new supply of oil could be consecrated. Hence, this tradition explains why Hanukkah is held for eight days. An alternative tradition (Shabbat 20a) explains that upon entering the Temple, the Maccabees found eight iron spears. They stuck candles on the spears and kindled them. In either case, both explanations are fanciful and were not suggested until centuries after the earliest historical accounts of the holiday.

Most likely the popular tradition of the oil cruse arose in an attempt to religiously redirect the central focus of Hanukkah away from the Maccabean dynasty which later became very corrupt. This would explain why Hanukkah is mentioned only on rare instances in the Talmud. The Talmud grew out of the Pharisaic tradition, which was at greatly at odds with that of the Sadducees who aligned themselves with the descendants of the Maccabees.

This would also have proven to be politically expedient during the first century A.D. Israel was under Roman rule, and it would not have exhibited national prudence to continue to emphasize the victorious, Maccabean-rebellion side of the holiday. The Jewish historian, Josephus (first century A.D.), knew the holiday as the Feast of Lights (*Antiquities of the Jews* 12.7.7) centuries before the oil-cruse tradition was suggested.

■ ■ THE MODERN OBSERVANCE

Over the past 2,000 years, Hanukkah observance has continued to develop. Many beautiful traditions exist today that remember the Lord's deliverance through the faithful Maccabees.

A Time of Lights

In the Home

The principal ceremony of Hanukkah is the lighting of candles each evening in the home and synagogue. Their light may not be used for any practical purposes, only for the celebration of the holiday. The Hanukkah menorah (candelabra), called a *hanukkiyah*, holds eight candles (one for each night of Hanukkah). An additional place (usually in the center and lifted higher than the others) is reserved for a ninth candle, called the *shammash*, or "servant" candle. It is used to light the other candles. Each night, one additional light is lit, using the servant candle, until all eight are lit on the eighth night of Hanukkah. By tradition, they are lit from left to right, and a special blessing is said before and after the lights are kindled thanking God for His deliverance. The Hanukkah menorah is placed in the front window of the house so that all who pass by may see the lights and be reminded of the meaning of Hanukkah.

In Israel

On the eve of Hanukkah, marathon runners are sent to the village of Modin, the initial site of the ancient Maccabean revolt. Flaming freedom torches are lit from the Hanukkah menorah there and are carried by the runners to Jerusalem where a procession is held at the Western Wall of the Temple to kindle the great menorah. This ceremony is not only a reminder of freedom but represents the spirit of martyrdom which made it possible.

A Time of Gifts

Hanukkah is a time of gifts. Especially in America, Hanukkah has been tremendously affected by Christmas because of its proximity. To counteract the strong influence, the exchange of gifts has become a regular part of twentieth-century Hanukkah observance.

An earlier tradition, preserved from Eastern Europe, involves the custom of giving Hanukkah *gelt* (Yiddish for "money"). On the fifth night of

Hanukkah, parents and grandparents gather the children and give them coins.

Hanukkah is also a special time of the year for *tzedekah* (charity). Because the blind cannot enjoy lighting the Hanukkah lights, the major ceremony of the holiday, special contributions are often given to charities for the blind.

A Time of Games

Hanukkah is a time for games. Adults often enjoy playing cards. The practice of playing games of chance was protested by various rabbis through the centuries, but the tradition remains today.

The most popular children's game for Hanukkah is the *dreidel* (Yiddish) or *sivivon* (Hebrew). It is a four-sided top with one Hebrew letter on each of its sides. The letters are the first letters of the words in the phrase *Nes Gadol Hayah Sham*, "A great miracle happened there." In Israel, the last word is changed to "here" since it was in Israel that the events of Hanukkah occurred. Each player puts a coin, nut, or foil-covered chocolate coin in the "pot" and takes turns spinning the top. If the Hebrew letter *nun* lands up, nothing happens. If *gimel*, the player wins the whole pot. If *hay*, the player wins half the pot. If *shin*, the player loses one coin to the pot.

A Time of Foods

Hanukkah is a time of food. Hanukkah parties are often arranged with friends and family to celebrate the lighting of the candles.

Two major schools of tradition developed during the past 1,900 years of Jewish dispersion. *Ashkenazic* traditions developed in the Jewish communities in Eastern and Central Europe. *Sephardic* traditions arose among the Jewish communities scattered throughout Spain, Northern Africa, and the Middle East.

During Hanukkah, it is customary to eat foods fried in oil as a reminder of the oil-cruse tradition. Ashkenazic Jews frequently eat *latkes*, or potato pancakes fried in oil. Sephardic Jews preserve the tradition of eating *sufganiyot*, or deep-fried doughnuts. These jelly-filled doughnuts, sprinkled with powdered sugar, are a favorite Hanukkah delicacy.

A Time of Singing

Hanukkah is a time of singing. A popular Ashkenazic tradition is the singing of *Maoz Tzur*, or "Mighty Rock," which praises God as Israel's deliverer. It was written in the thirteenth century by an unknown German poet and takes its name from Isaiah 26:4. A popular Sephardic tradition is the reciting of Psalm 30 after the lighting of the candles.

 THE BIBLICAL CONNECTION

The Pattern of Scripture

Although the fanciful legend of the oil cruse exists today, it provides no credible answers as to why Hanukkah is celebrated for eight days and why it is celebrated with lights. However, one need look no further than Scripture to find the pattern for Hanukkah.

Why Eight Days?

According to the Talmud (Megillat Taanit 9), it took eight days to rebuild the altar and, therefore, Hanukkah is celebrated for eight days. While the altar may or may not have taken eight days to rebuild (the earliest sources for Hanukkah do not say), a much more solid basis exists for the pattern of observance.

In Scripture, an eight-day period was always the pattern of dedication. That is, the object to be dedicated was set aside (sanctified) for seven days, and then on the eighth day it was holy to the Lord. Such was the case with firstborn animals consecrated to God (Ex. 22:30; Lev. 22:27). Hebrew males were also circumcised on the eighth day (Lev. 12:3). The original altar in the Temple was sanctified for seven days, and on the eighth it was holy (Ex. 29:37). The dedication of the rebuilt Temple after Babylonian captivity took place during Passover (Ezra 6:16-22), which in conjunction with the Feast of Unleavened Bread lasted for eight days. Further, the future altar of the millennial Temple will be consecrated on the eighth day (Ezek. 43:26-27).

But an even closer parallel to Hanukkah was the situation of King Hezekiah's day. His father, wicked King Ahaz, had desecrated the Temple of the living God with altars and sacrifices to the Assyrian gods (2 Ki. 16:10-18; 2 Chr. 28:21-25). When godly King Hezekiah came to the throne, he cleansed the Temple and rededicated it to the Lord after eight days (2 Chr. 29:16-17).

But there is further reason that Hanukkah is celebrated for eight days — it was directly patterned after the Feast of Tabernacles. The Feast of Tabernacles was a seven-day feast followed by a sabbath of rest. Concerning Hanukkah, Jewish history records:

> And they kept eight days with gladness, as in the feast of the tabernacles, remembering that not long afore they had held the feast of tabernacles, when they wandered in the mountains and dens like beasts. Therefore they bare branches, and fair boughs, and palms also, and sang psalms unto him that had given them good success in cleansing his place (2 Macc. 10:6-7).

So, originally, Hanukkah was almost a second observance of Tabernacles, in much the same way that Hezekiah instituted a second observance of Passover when the people were not able to keep the first one (2 Chr. 30; cf. Num. 9:10-11). This explains why the Hallel (Psalms 113-118), which was originally sung only at Tabernacles, is still sung in the synagogue Hanukkah service today. The Maccabees "sang psalms" (2 Macc. 10:7) as in Tabernacles.

Why Lights?

The fact that Hanukkah is patterned after Tabernacles also provides the meaning for the emphasis on lights. When Solomon dedicated the first Temple to the Lord, he did so at the Feast of Tabernacles (2 Chr. 5:3). That dedication was accompanied by the coming of the Shekinah glory to the Temple and the divine lighting of the fire upon the sacrificial altar (2 Chr. 7:1). As a result, the Feast of Tabernacles later developed an impressive light celebration each night in the Temple. Since Hanukkah celebrated the relighting of the fire on the purified altar and was patterned after Tabernacles, the emphasis upon light was borrowed quite naturally as well.

The Prophecy of Daniel

The Hebrew Scriptures do not directly mention Hanukkah since the holiday was not instituted until after the Old Testament was complete. But even though Hanukkah is not mentioned by name, the events of Hanukkah were prophesied centuries beforehand by the Hebrew prophet, Daniel.

Daniel saw an awesome vision (Dan. 8:1-12). He saw a ram with two horns (the Medo-Persian empire) pushing so that no beasts could stand before it. Then a goat (Greece) appeared in the west and moved so quickly that its feet did not touch the ground. A very noticeable horn (Alexander the Great) was between its eyes. The goat (Greece) crashed into the ram (Medo-Persia) with incredible fury and broke the two horns from its head, all but killing it. No sooner had the goat (Greece) become great, when its large horn was broken, allowing four smaller horns (Alexander's generals) to replace it. Then, amazingly, a little horn (Antiochus) came up from one of the four and became exceedingly powerful. It cast down some of the stars (righteous Jews) and stamped on them. It even magnified itself to the Prince of the starry host, took away the sacrifices, and cast down His sanctuary (the Temple in Jerusalem).

Several chapters later, Daniel again prophesied of this coming Syrian persecution and the courage of God's people: "But the people who know their God shall be strong, and carry out great exploits. And those of the people who understand shall instruct many; yet for many days they shall fall by sword and flame, by captivity and plundering" (Dan. 11:32-33).

The Preaching of Jesus (Jn. 10:22)

It is only natural that, during Hanukkah (the celebration of freedom from foreign oppression), thoughts of national deliverance would again be aroused. In the day of Jesus, Israel was looking for the ultimate deliverer, the Messiah himself, who would overthrow Roman rule. If He were to deliver the Jewish nation, they would never fall under Gentile dominion again. He would usher in the golden messianic age, making it possible for the Shekinah glory to return to the Temple as in the days of Solomon's dedication of the Temple.

With this thought on their minds, a group of Jewish inquirers came to Jesus. It was Hanukkah, and Jesus was walking along Solomon's colonnade (the pillared walkway in the Temple). He was celebrating Hanukkah in the same Temple that had been cleansed and rededicated only a few generations earlier. These inquirers asked: "How long do You keep us in doubt? If You are the Christ [Messiah], tell us plainly" (Jn. 10:24). Indeed He had clearly shown that He was the Messiah and verified it with many miracles. They had rejected Him because He consistently failed to meet their messianic expectations. They were looking for a military messiah, one who was only a great human leader. Therefore, Jesus tried to broaden their narrow understanding on the deity of the Messiah by His significant assertion, "I and My Father are one" (Jn. 10:30). But this drove them into such a rage that they sought to stone Him. Actually, earlier in the same passage, when Jesus claimed to be the "good shepherd" (Jn. 10:11), He was also identifying with the Shepherd of Israel (Ps. 80:1; Isa. 40:11; Ezek. 34:12-23) in a similar, albeit less direct, claim to deity. But there could be no new occasion of Hanukkah (the overthrow of Gentile rule), for the nation was still blind in their rejection.

The Faithful Martyrs (Heb. 11:35)

The writer of Hebrews, in citing examples of great faith, mentioned the godly believers who stood against Antiochus Epiphanes. He recorded: "Others were tortured, not accepting deliverance, that they might obtain a better resurrection . . . of whom the world was not worthy. They wandered in deserts and mountains, in dens and caves of the earth. And all these, having obtained a good testimony through faith, did not receive the promise" (Heb. 11:35-39).

The Hanukkah story reveals the names of some of these nameless martyrs listed in the Book of Hebrews. In their fervent zeal, Eleazar, Hannah, and her sons were stellar examples of faithfulness to God as they steadfastly sought to "obtain a better resurrection."

The Name of Matthew

Matthew, the Levite and follower of Jesus (Mt. 9:9; Lk. 5:27), was undoubtedly named after Mattathias, the Levite hero of Israel who lived a century and a half before his birth. The name Matthew (English) is taken from Mattathias (Greek) which is taken from Matityahu (Hebrew).

The Date of Christmas

Many have suggested a connection between Hanukkah and Christmas since both celebrations fall on the 25th of the month (Kislev/December). Although the Bible records the birth of the Messiah, no biblical basis exists for the date or observance of the Messiah's birthday. In fact, for more than three centuries, the early Church viewed the celebration of birthdays as a heathen custom.

Yet, the dates of Hanukkah and Christmas *are* connected. Zeus was seen as the incarnation of the sun. Together with his goddess-mother, Rhea (the Queen of Heaven), they formed the Greek version of the mother/child cult founded in Babylon. Antiochus chose the 25th of the month to desecrate the Temple with his pagan sacrifice because it was the birthday of Zeus. It was the winter solstice, when days began to lengthen. Sun-worshiping pagans, therefore, celebrated December 25 as the birthday of the new sun.

To the sun-worshiping Romans, Zeus was known as Jupiter. He was the son of Saturn and Ops. He was the supreme Roman deity and the father of the other pagan gods. December 17-24 was called *Saturnalia* (in honor of Saturn) and celebrated with unrestrained license. The Romans celebrated December 25th (the birthday of Zeus/Jupiter) as *Dies Natalis Invicti Solis*, "the Day of the Nativity of the Unconquered Sun."

In the fourth century A.D., the Roman Church chose December 25 as the day to celebrate "Christ's Mass," a special mass in honor of Christ's birth. It was part of a concerted effort to "Christianize" pagan Roman rites so that all peoples of the empire could be brought into the Roman Church.

For centuries, many segments of Christianity condemned the observance of December 25 as sun worship. A. H. Newman writes: "Christian preachers of the West and the Nearer East protested against the unseemly frivolity with which Christ's birthday was celebrated, while Christians of Mesopotamia accused their Western brethren of idolatry and sun-worship for adopting as Christian this pagan festival. Yet the festival rapidly gained acceptance and became, at last, so firmly established that even the Protestant revolution of the sixteenth century was not able to dislodge it" (*The New Schaff-Herzog Encyclopedia of Religious Knowledge*, p. 48).

◼ THE FUTURE FULFILLMENT

Throughout the ages, Gentile nations have been obsessed with desecrating the Temple Mount, the footstool of our God. It was there that Antiochus erected the image of Zeus. It was there that the Roman emperor Hadrian constructed a temple to Jupiter. Today, the Temple Mount is desecrated with shrines to Allah, the god of the crescent moon.

This pattern is to continue, as another Hanukkah is yet future. Scripture teaches that the events of Hanukkah are merely a shadow of events at the end of this age. Daniel prophesied that "many" within Israel will again enter into a covenant or security agreement with a Gentile ruler (Dan. 9:27). This wicked ruler is known as Armilus by Jewish theologians and

Antichrist by Christians. The confirmation of the covenant will start the clock ticking for the seven-year period known as the Seventieth Week of Daniel. This covenant, called a covenant with "death" and "Sheol" (Isa. 28:15), will be the outward sign of the apostasy of the nation. In their blindness, they will turn to a Gentile leader for peace instead of to the one true God.

At midpoint, three and one-half years later, Jerusalem will be captured and oppressed by the Gentiles (Lk. 21:20; Rev. 11:2). Then Antichrist will be revealed for who he is; he will declare himself to be god and demand the worship of the world (2 Th. 2:4; Rev. 13:12-15)). Like Antiochus Epiphanes, he will desecrate the rebuilt Temple with his idolatrous image, rendering it utterly desolate. The Messiah said in reference to this: "Therefore when you see the 'abomination of desolation,' spoken of by Daniel the prophet, standing in the holy place . . . then let those who are in Judea flee to the mountains" (Mt. 24:15-16).

The line will again be drawn — either assimilate or be annihilated. Many will fall away (apostatize) and bow down (2 Th. 2:3), but the faithful within Israel will flee to the mountains and wilderness. Many of the faithful will lose their lives (Mt. 24:22) as the Antichrist vents his wrath on the people of God (Rev. 12:13-17). That time of great tribulation (Mt. 24:21) will be like nothing the nation has ever experienced (Jer. 30:7; Dan. 12:1).

But God, who is faithful, will again remember His people Israel. He will send the Messiah to deliver the remnant of Israel and raise up a new Temple (Zech. 6:12) to which the Shekinah glory will return (Isa. 4:5; Ezek. 43:1-6). And in that day, "The remnant of Israel, And such as have escaped of the house of Jacob, Will never again depend on him who defeated them [Antichrist], But will depend on the LORD, the Holy One of Israel, in truth" (Isa. 10:20).

CONCLUSION

Hanukkah stands as a heroic reminder of courageous and enduring faith in God. Many were martyred, "not accepting deliverance, that they might obtain a better resurrection" (Heb. 11:35). Others did great exploits for their God. And it is that one quality, faith, that God is looking for in men and women today. He is pleased with those who steadfastly put their trust in Him, for "without faith it is impossible to please Him" (Heb. 11:6). The Word of God relates of Abraham, that great man of faith, that "he believed in the LORD, and He accounted it to him for righteousness" (Gen. 15:6).

But Hanukkah is also a reminder of the faithfulness of God. Satan, through Antiochus Epiphanes, had planned to destroy God's Word and His people through assimilation and annihilation. Had he been successful, there would have been no more Jewish people, no Messiah to come, and most tragically of all, no Calvary. Men and women would be forever lost in sin, without hope. And so a great miracle did happen there. It is not a cruse of oil but God's faithfulness to His people and His messianic promise that continue to give true significance to Hanukkah today.

פורים

"So they called these days Purim, after the name Pur"
(Est. 9:26).

Purim —
The Feast of Lots

Kevin L. Howard

Anti-Semitism is hardly a modern phenomenon. For untold centuries, Israel's embittered enemies have, with craft and cruel hatred, plotted the annihilation of the sons of Jacob. Yet, the wayside of human history is strewn with the debris of Israel's detractors. They have plotted, schemed, and counseled together, but in the end their treachery has only brought about their own demise. Their only lasting achievement has been an occasion for a new holiday on the Hebrew calendar. Such was the case with Pharaoh when the Lord instituted Passover. Such was the case with the defeat of Antiochus Epiphanes and the resulting feast of Hanukkah. Such was also the case with the defeat of Hitler, which paved the way for the emergence of the modern State of Israel and its annual Independence Day celebration. It was also true of the Jewish feast of Purim and its institution in ancient Persia.

THE HISTORICAL BACKGROUND

The Meaning of Purim

Purim is the Hebrew word for "lots" in remembrance of the *pur* ("lot") cast by the wicked Haman to determine the month and day on which the Jewish people were to be killed throughout the mighty Persian Empire. Ironically, the lots that were thrown for Israel's destruction actually set the date for a new national celebration.

Known as "The Feast of Esther" and in antiquity as "Mordecai's Day" (2 Macc. 15:36), Purim commemorates the deliverance of God's people at the hands of Esther and Mordecai.

The Time of Purim

Purim is a late winter feast (late February or March), the last feast of the biblical year. It occurs on the 14th day of Adar, the twelfth Hebrew month (or, in a leap year, on the 14th day of Adar Sheni, the thirteenth month), exactly one month before Passover.

In Jerusalem today, Purim is celebrated on Adar 15, one day later than in the rest of the world. This is in commemoration of the Jews in the ancient Persian capital of Shushan who did not rest from fighting their enemies until the following day (Est. 9:18). Adar 15 is therefore known as *Shushan Purim*.

The Record of Purim

Purim is an additional feast, one that was instituted centuries after the time of Moses. As such, Purim is nowhere to be found in the divinely given feasts of Leviticus 23. But despite this fact, Purim is a biblical feast and the best-known Jewish holiday added since the time of Moses. The record of its historical background and observance is preserved in the Bible in the Book of Esther.

The authorship of the Book of Esther is not certain, but Mordecai has been traditionally viewed as its author. This seems most likely since it was Mordecai who communicated the institution of Purim to the Jewish people throughout the Persian Empire by way of official letter (Est. 9:20, 29). Mordecai was also intimately acquainted with the Persian laws and culture woven throughout the Book of Esther.

The Heroes of Purim

In 538 B.C., the majority of Persian Jewry chose to remain in Persia rather than return to their homeland under the leadership of Zerubbabel. For more than fifty years they continued to flourish in the comfort of dispersion rather than suffer the hardships involved in returning to Israel. From all outward appearances, they were well-integrated, even semi-assimilated, into Persian society; that is, until the days of Esther.

From this well-integrated Jewish Diaspora (dispersion) came Esther and Mordecai, the two towering heroes of Purim. To avoid Persian anti-Semitism, they masked their Jewishness from the public eye. Esther's given Persian name was derived from the pagan goddess, Ishtar, and

Mordecai's from the Babylonian god, Marduk, very similar to the name changes of Daniel and his three Hebrew companions living in the Babylonian court (Dan. 1:7). However, beneath their Persian social veneer, Esther and Mordecai were both strongly nationalistic and fiercely devoted to the God of Israel.

Esther's Hebrew name, Hadassah, meaning "myrtle," was a fitting name indeed in light of her tremendous beauty (Est. 2:7). Her parents died when she was young, and her cousin, Mordecai, adopted and raised her as his daughter.

Mordecai held a high office in the Medo-Persian court (the world power of his day), giving him access to the palace (Est. 2:5, 11) and necessitating his presence in the king's gate (Est. 2:20-21). Yet, Mordecai maintained a strong Hebrew identity. He was the distinguished "son of Jair, the son of Shimei, the son of Kish, a Benjamite" (Est. 2:5), of the exact same lineage as King Saul.

This fact created an interesting backdrop for the story. Mordecai's enemy, Haman, was an Agagite (Est. 3:1), a descendant of Agag, the king of the Amalekites during Saul's reign (1 Sam. 15:8). The Amalekite people were descendants of Amalek, the grandson of Esau (Gen. 36:12). As bitter enemies of Israel, they carried on the ancient strife between Jacob and Esau. In the day of Moses and Joshua, the Amalekites treacherously attacked the unarmed Israelites as they passed through the Sinai. The Lord never forgot their blind, inbred hatred, and pronounced a curse to "blot out the remembrance of Amalek from under heaven" (Dt. 25:19; cf. Ex. 17:14, 16; Num. 24:20).

King Saul had been commanded by the Lord to utterly destroy all the Amalekites. Had he only been obedient, the threat of annihilation at the hand of Haman would not have been possible. However, the descendants of Saul and Agag met again almost six centuries later and were once again engaged in mortal conflict.

The Origin of Purim

The setting of the Book of Esther was the king's palace in Shushan, the Persian capital, located just north of the Persian Gulf in what today is modern Iran. The events took place during the reign of Ahasuerus (identified by historians as Xerxes I, 486-465 B.C.). The mighty Persian Empire was at the zenith of its power and glory with its 127 provinces stretching from "India to Ethiopia" (Est. 1:1).

Insubordination by the Queen (Esther 1)

During the third year of his reign, Ahasuerus held a lavish, six-month feast for the nobility among his provinces. He desired to impress them with his wealth and majestic palace. Indeed his opulent palace must have been overwhelmingly impressive with its stunning pavilions of "white and blue linen curtains fastened with cords of fine linen and purple on silver rods and marble pillars; and the couches were of gold and silver on a mosaic pavement of alabaster, turquoise, and white and black marble" (Est. 1:6).

Immediately following this elaborate feast, Ahasuerus held a seven-day feast open to all his subjects. On the seventh and final day, while drunk, he ordered Queen Vashti to display her great beauty before his princes and men of renown in attendance. Because of strict Persian law, which forbade women to be seen unveiled by strangers (much like Islamic law today), she refused his command in order to preserve her reputation. However, in doing so, Vashti created a national crisis. Her example threatened the Persian honor of the king and the social dominance of the men of Persia. Ahasuerus was incensed with her insubordination and conferred with his princes. His princes asserted that the only possible course of action was for Vashti to "come no more before King Ahasuerus" and to "give her royal position to another who is better than she" (Est. 1:19). And so, Vashti was deposed.

Inauguration of a New Queen (Esther 2:1-18)

While the removal of the queen resolved the pressing crisis, it created the need for a new queen. So the king appointed officers throughout the provinces, and many fair maidens were brought into the "house of the women" as potential candidates for queen. Among them was Esther. She immediately found favor with the keeper of the women and was given preferential treatment with the best accommodations in the house. King Ahasuerus, too, was captivated by Esther and "loved Esther more than all the other women, and she obtained grace and favor in his sight more than all the virgins" (Est. 2:17). And so, Esther became the queen of Persia.

Intrigue in the King's Court (Esther 2:19-23)

One day, in the course of his official duties at the king's gate, Mordecai overheard two rebellious chamberlains plotting the assassination of King Ahasuerus. Their planned bloody coup was quickly reported to Esther, and an immediate investigation was launched by the king. The matter was verified, and the conspirators were hanged. As a result, Mordecai's heroic deed and faithfulness to the king were recorded in the royal chronicles of Persia.

Intentions for Evil (Esther 3)

Shortly thereafter, a tragic appointment was made in the Persian royal court. A prince named Haman was promoted to the position of prime minister over all the other princes, answering only to the king. At the king's command, all were to bow and do obeisance (as homage to a god) in Haman's presence. For the devout Mordecai, idolatry was unthinkable. He worshiped only the one true God. When questioned by the other royal officers as to why he daily disobeyed the king's command, he explained his Jewishness.

When the matter was told to Haman, he determined to kill not only Mordecai but all Jews everywhere. If one would not bow, it was clear that none of the Jewish people would bow before him. His inflated ego and honor were at stake. Having purposed to annihilate the Jewish people, Haman cast lots to gain direction from the Persian gods for the best date for the planned massacre. The lots fell to Adar 13, giving Haman some eleven months to work out the details of his demonic plan.

Haman petitioned King Ahasuerus to obtain the needed authorization for his edict. He reported that a troublesome people existed within the Persian kingdom. They were dispersed as a foreign and evil element throughout the empire, they held incompatible laws, and they rebelled against the laws of the king. As he presented his case, Haman outlined his final solution for this hated people. He proposed an edict calling for their destruction. In return he offered 10,000 talents (more than ten million ounces) of silver to the royal treasury. It is not clear whether this enormous sum was to compensate for the significant economic loss to the empire or to defray the extensive military costs for such an operation. Apparently, Haman counted on recovering his bribe from the seized property of the Jewish victims. Because of his great confidence in Haman, King Ahasuerus removed the royal signet ring and gave it to Haman, granting him full authority to carry out his insidious plot. So Haman sent the evil edict, hastened by the command of the king, "into all the king's provinces, to destroy, to kill, and to annihilate all the Jews, both young and old, little children and women, in one day, on the thirteenth day of the twelfth month, which is the month of Adar, and to plunder their possessions" (Est. 3:13).

Intercession by Esther (Esther 4 & 5)

When word of the sinister decree came to Mordecai, he tore his clothes in bitter anguish, put on sackcloth, and covered himself with ashes. Mordecai related the dire news to Esther and gave her a copy of the edict. He insistently pled with her to intercede before the king on behalf of her people.

This posed a grave dilemma for Esther. She feared to approach the king. According to Persian law, if anyone came uninvited into the inner court of the king, he would be killed. The only possible exception was for the king to put forth his golden scepter to stay the execution. But Esther had not been summoned by the king for thirty days. The strong possibility existed that she would forfeit her life for such a brazen breach of Persian law. Mordecai replied: "If you remain completely silent at this time, relief and deliverance will arise for the Jews from another place . . . . who knows whether you have come to the kingdom for such a time as this?" (Est. 4:14).

Esther was persuaded and requested only that Mordecai gather the Jewish people of Shushan and fast for three days before she petitioned the king. Courageously she resolved, "So I will go to the king, which is against the law; and if I perish, I perish!" (Est. 4:16).

On the third day of her fast, Esther donned her royal apparel and stood in the inner court of King Ahasuerus. When the astonished king saw her in the court, he extended his golden scepter to spare her life. Seeing her great distress and desperate action, the king promised to grant any request within his power to fulfill. Ingeniously, Esther delayed her request and instead asked that the king and Haman come to a banquet prepared in their honor.

At the banquet, the king again asked, "What is your petition? It shall be granted you" (Est. 5:6). Not wanting to rush the decision, especially since it concerned the king's most trusted government advisor, Esther again invited the king and Haman to a banquet on the following night. Ideal circumstances were required for her difficult petition.

The egotistical Haman was elated that he had once again been invited to a private royal banquet. He viewed it as the pinnacle of his career and rushed home to boast to his wife and friends. However, the smallest needle has a way of bursting the largest balloon. As he passed through the king's gate, he met Mordecai who again stubbornly refused to bow. Haman's deep-seated hatred flared as he complained to his friends: "Yet all this avails me nothing, so long as I see Mordecai the Jew sitting at the king's gate" (Est. 5:13). His friends counseled him to build a 75-foot gallows and hang Mordecai the next morning. This would allow Haman to fully enjoy his banquet in the evening.

Insomnia for the King (Esther 6)

That night the king could not sleep. More than just a case of too much Turkish coffee, his insomnia was divinely appointed. Being the vain monarch that he was, Ahasuerus called for the royal chronicles to be read so that his brilliant achievements and mighty exploits could be rehearsed in his ears. As the records were read, Mordecai's faithfulness in foiling the attempt on his life was recounted. King Ahasuerus was very troubled when he realized that Mordecai had gone unrewarded for such a great deed.

The next morning, the king noticed Haman waiting in the outer court to gain a meeting with him. Haman was waiting for permission to hang Mordecai upon the newly constructed gallows. The king summoned Haman and asked, "What shall be done for the man whom the king delights to honor?" (Est. 6:6). Thinking that the king was referring to him, Haman answered: "Let a royal robe be brought which the king has worn, and a horse on which the king has ridden, which has a royal crest placed on its head . . . . Then parade him on horseback through the city square, and proclaim before him" (Est. 6:8-9). The king then commanded Haman to quickly perform that honor to Mordecai and to personally lead Mordecai through the streets on horseback. Haman was horror-stricken in his utter humiliation, but things were to sour further in his plot against the Jewish people.

Incrimination of the Perpetrator (Esther 7)

At the banquet, Esther finally made her petition known to the king. She pled for King Ahasuerus to save her and her people from impending destruction. This was a surprising revelation indeed, since the king was not aware that Esther was Jewish. The angered Ahasuerus immediately arose and demanded to know the identity of the enemy. Pointing to Haman, Esther answered, "The adversary and enemy is this wicked Haman!" (Est. 7:6). In a heated rage, the king stormed from the banquet hall to contemplate his actions. As he did so, the blood drained from Haman's face, for he knew that his life was in certain danger. In the thrashings of his terror, he threw himself on the queen's couch to beg for mercy. But at that moment the king returned and mistook Haman's actions for violence against his queen. The time for talk was past. King Ahasuerus ordered the executioners to cover Haman's face and hang him on the gallows prepared for Mordecai.

Initiation of New Decrees (Esther 8:1-9:16)

In the wake of Haman's demise, Mordecai was promoted to Haman's position and given the royal signet ring. But the Persian law still stood which called for the destruction of Esther's people. So she again risked her life by going before the king to beg for the deliverance of her people. However, a difficulty existed — laws within the Medo-Persian government could never be repealed. Therefore, the king commanded Mordecai and Esther to draft a decree to the provinces and seal it with his signet granting the Jewish people the right of self-defense against their aggressors. Normally, as in Islamic countries today, to take a life even accidentally would mean the forfeiture of one's own life or payment of huge sums of compensation to the survivors.

When the fateful Adar 13 arrived, the Jews of Persia fought for their lives. Fearing the exalted Mordecai, the provincial rulers aided the Jewish people under their local authority. But anti-Semitism was especially ingrained in the capital city where particularly fierce fighting carried over until the next day. When it was finished, the enemies of God's people were killed — 75,000 in the provinces, 800 in Shushan, and the ten sons of

Haman were hanged on the gallows lest there be blood revenge.

Institution of Purim (Esther 9:17-32)

To remember God's mighty deliverance, Mordecai carefully recorded the events and "sent letters to all the Jews, near and far, who were in all the provinces . . . that they should celebrate yearly the fourteenth and fifteenth days of the month of Adar" (Est. 9:20-21). The feast was called Purim, for Haman had "cast Pur, (that is, the lot), to consume them and destroy them" (Est. 9:24). And so Purim became a feast for Israel, a day of "feasting and joy, of sending presents to one another and gifts to the poor" (Est. 9:22), so that the memory of Purim would never cease throughout all generations.

  # THE MODERN OBSERVANCE

Being instituted after the Mosaic Law, Purim is considered a minor holiday, and no restrictions are placed upon working. Even in the Book of Esther, no religious ceremonies were observed other than a time of "feasting and joy, of sending presents to one another and gifts to the poor" (Esther 9:22). With no other details given for its observance, many warm Purim traditions have developed over the past 2,500 years.

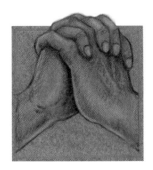

A Time of Remembrance

The Fast of Esther

Sometime after the institution of Purim, Adar 13 also became connected to the holiday and was celebrated as the "Fast of Esther." The original fast requested by Esther was three days in duration (Est. 4:16) and was kept near Passover, some eleven months earlier than Purim (Est. 3:12). Since the fast is not strictly commanded, very few actually keep it today.

The Scroll of Esther

The principal ceremony of Purim is the reading of the Book of Esther in the synagogue. A handwritten scroll of Esther is read at the beginning of Purim, just after the evening service. It is also read again the next day during the morning synagogue service. Through these readings, the listeners relive the miraculous events of Purim.

The Book of Esther is known as a *megillah* ("scroll") in Hebrew. It is the best-known of the five books of the Hebrew Bible which are known as "scrolls." These scrolls are short and are read on different holidays — The Song of Solomon (Passover), Ruth (Feast of Weeks), Lamentations (Tisha B'Av), Ecclesiastes (Tabernacles), and Esther (Purim).

During Purim, the divine command to blot out the name of Amalek is taken literally. When Haman's name is read from the scroll of Esther, it is met by a thunderous roar of clapping, stamping feet, booing, and the grinding noise of twirling noisemakers. These hand-held noisemakers, called *groggers*, were developed especially for drowning out Haman's name. Each grogger consists of a noisemaker which twirls at the end of a handle.

Some other interesting methods for "erasing" Haman's name existed in the past. One tradition was to write Haman's name on the soles of the shoes, and as the feet were stamped during the reading of the scroll, Haman's name was literally erased. Another tradition, known as "beating Haman," involved building an effigy (likeness) of Haman which was then hanged and burned. However, this custom was largely abandoned in the Middle Ages when anti-Semitic slanders were leveled that the Jewish people burned a figure of Jesus on the cross during Purim and served as a basis for attacks upon them.

The Half Shekel

Before the reading of the scroll, it is customary to pass a plate in the synagogue in remembrance of the ancient injunction for each Israelite male to donate one-half shekel annually toward the maintenance of the Temple (Ex. 30:13). Usually, one to three silver coins (such as a silver dollar or half-dollar) are on the plate that is circulated. Each worshiper places a gift of money on the plate so that the silver coins become his. The coins are picked up and immediately donated back to the plate, thus fulfilling the ancient command. The collection is usually given to charity in fulfillment of Mordecai's command to give "gifts to the poor" during Purim (Est. 9:22).

A Time of Gifts

Purim is a time of "sending presents to one another and gifts to the poor" (Est. 9:22). The practice (known as *mishloah manot*) of sending portions of food delicacies to friends is a widespread Purim tradition. This outward expression of joy usually involves the sending of a plate full of cake, pastries, fruit, and nuts by the hand of a child to friends and relatives.

It is also customary to give charity to at least two needy individuals during Purim so that they may be able to enjoy the festival. Even small children participate in giving several coins to charity.

A Time of Foods

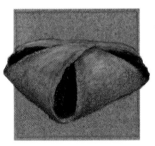

Purim is a time of special holiday foods and "feasting" (Est. 9:17). The most popular food for Purim today is known as *Hamantashen*. Hamantashen are delicious triangular pastries, filled with poppy seed (or prune) filling. Their name is derived from two German words — *mohn* ("poppy seed") and *taschen* ("pockets"). According to tradition, Hamantashen are reminiscent of Haman's three-cornered hat. Hamantashen are often served for breakfast on Purim.

Another festive dish for Purim is known as *kreplach*. The noodle-like kreplach are made from triangular pieces of dough, stuffed with a chopped meat and minced-onion filling, and served in a thick, steaming soup.

Traditionally, a festive meal, known as the Purim *Seudah*, is held late in the afternoon and draws friends and family together for the close of the joyous Purim holiday.

A Time of Gladness

Purim is a time of rejoicing and gladness, the merriest holiday on the Hebrew calendar today. The rabbis of the Talmud taught that one should get so caught up (and some even encouraged drinking) in the joy of Purim that he is no longer able to tell the difference between "cursed be Haman" and "blessed be Mordecai." So, during Purim one may hear the familiar Hebrew phrase *Ad de lo yada* ("until not able to distinguish").

As part of the Purim joy, the holiday is often celebrated with masquerades, costumes, and carnivals. Traditionally, masquerading was banned under Jewish law because it often involved wearing clothes of the opposite sex, a practice strictly forbidden in the Bible (Dt. 22:5). Because of Purim's great joy, masquerading was permitted by the rabbis and is a universal Purim custom today.

In Israel, the most well-known Purim event is the *Adloyada* parade and carnival which is held in Tel Aviv each year.

 THE BIBLICAL CONNECTION

The Defeat of God's Enemies

The underlying principle of Purim is found in the Abrahamic Covenant. God promised Abraham: "I will make you a great nation; I will bless you And make your name great; And you shall be a blessing. I will bless those who bless you, And I will curse him who curses you; And in you all the families of the earth shall be blessed" (Gen. 12:2-3). In a general sense, God deals with mankind in the same way that they deal with the sons of Abraham. One's attitude toward the *sons* of Abraham is reflective of one's attitude toward the *God* of Abraham. To curse Israel, whom God has blessed, is to set oneself in direct opposition to God. This is not to say that Israel is always righteous, for she is not. However, to hate Israel is to hate the God who created her. The Lord says concerning the Jewish people, "He who touches you touches the apple of His eye" (Zech. 2:8).

In light of this, the Abrahamic Covenant exhibits something of a "boomerang effect." God blesses men to the exact degree that they bless the sons of Israel (especially Israel's Greater Son, Jesus), and the curses that are hurled against Israel He brings back upon the heads of her enemies.

This explains the irony of Haman. Haman built the gallows for Mordecai, but he himself was hanged on it. Haman sought to solidify his position, but his position was given instead to Mordecai. Haman sought to kill Mordecai's people, but he, his whole family, and all those who hated the Jews were killed instead. Haman sought to wipe out the worship of the one true God which prevented men from bowing to him, but instead, "many of the people of the land became Jews, because fear of the Jews fell upon them" (Est. 8:17).

The path of anti-Semitism is a well-worn path that always leads to the destruction of its traveler. The Hamans of history and this present hour are many. Even as the fate of Pharaoh, Antiochus Epiphanes, Hitler, Nasser, Khomeini (whose name actually was "Haman" in Farsi), so, too, will be the fate of Qadafi, Arafat, Assad, Saddam Hussein, and the host of others who dare to curse Israel and thereby the God of Abraham.

God has emphatically declared, "No weapon formed against you shall prosper, And every tongue which rises against you in judgment You shall condemn" (Isa. 54:17). But how emphatic is the statement of the Lord? He has decreed, "If those ordinances [the sun, moon, and stars] depart From before Me, says the LORD, Then the seed of Israel shall also cease From being a nation before Me forever" (Jer. 31:36).

The Deliverance of God's People

Yet, in the final analysis, Purim is far more than just the *defeat of God's enemies*; it is the *deliverance of God's people*.

God, through the prophet Daniel (Dan. 7), prophesied that there would arise four Gentile powers during Israel's history to exercise dominion over her. Each successive Gentile empire would be more hostile and anti-Semitic than the previous one. The Babylonian, Persian, and Greek empires oppressed Israel, but none will compare to the vicious hatred of the coming fourth and final empire, the revived Roman Empire under the leadership of the Antichrist. Daniel prophesied of that time: "And there shall be a time of trouble, Such as never was since there was a nation, Even to that time. And at that time your people shall be delivered" (Dan. 12:1). Israel clearly still awaits her final deliverance.

But how will that deliverance be accomplished? According to Scripture, deliverance is found only in a *Person* (the Lord), never in a *people*. Israel has no power to bring about her own deliverance. But it is exactly that humanistic, proud thinking that she can deliver herself that will prompt Israel to take her deliverance into her own hands and make a fatal covenant with the Antichrist. However, in the end, Israel will confess, "We have been with child, we have been in pain; We have, as it were, brought forth wind; We have not accomplished any deliverance in the earth, Nor have the inhabitants of the world fallen" (Isa. 26:18). Deliverance is found only in the Lord.

God has often delivered Israel in the past, but her *full* deliverance awaits the coming of the Deliverer (Rom. 11:26). For only when the Messiah (the rightful Heir to David's throne) comes will the yoke of Gentile oppression be forever removed from Israel's neck.

This truth is unknowingly proclaimed each Purim season as the Purim chorus is sung: *Utzu etzah, vetufar; dabru davar, velo yakum; ki immanuel.* It is actually the Hebrew text of the Lord's future warning to the Antichrist and his allied nations: "Take counsel together, but it will come to nothing; Speak the word, but it will not stand, For God is with us" (Isa. 8:10). Why will the plots against God's people always eventually fail? Because "God is with us," or literally in the Hebrew, because of *Immanuel.* But who is Immanuel? He is none other than Jesus, the Messiah of Israel, the same Immanuel whom Isaiah said would be born of a virgin (Isa. 7:14) and reign upon David's throne forever (Isa. 9:6-7). He will destroy Israel's greatest Haman, the Antichrist. He will deliver Israel from destruction. He will bind up the wounds of His people. It is He and He alone who delivers Israel.

But, of supreme significance, He is also the Deliverer of *all* who put their trust in Him. He offers deliverance from death at this very moment. God has said, "There is none who does good" (Ps. 53:3), and also, "The soul who sins shall die" (Ezek. 18:20). All men are sinners and are therefore under the curse of death. God's decree is irrevocable even as the law of the Medes and Persians was irrevocable. Sinful man deserves it, and God's perfect justice demands it. Yet, through the sacrificial death of the Messiah, God made a way of escape that does not negate His justice. A solitary question remains: "How shall we escape if we neglect so great a salvation?" (Heb. 2:3).

יובל

" 'That fiftieth year shall be a Jubilee to you; in it you shall neither sow nor reap what grows of its own accord, nor gather the grapes of your untended vine' " (Lev. 25:11).

The Jubilee Year

Kevin L. Howard

In addition to holy *days* and holy *weeks*, the Lord also designated holy *years* for Israel. Perhaps the most familiar of these is the Jubilee Year. However, the biblical details of the Jubilee Year are rarely discussed. Reliable writings on the subject are all but nonexistent.

Far too often the concept of the Jubilee Year is given very mystical applications, especially as the new millennium approaches. For example, the Pope is urgently calling for the year 2000 to be a "Jubilee Year" of ecumenical full fellowship between Christianity, Islam, and Judaism. He has called for simultaneous celebrations in Jerusalem and Rome. This is a very different concept of a Jubilee Year from that put forth by the Bible.

There has also been much speculation by date-setters who propose a host of conflicting dates for the next Jubilee Year in an attempt to predict the coming of the Messiah. In light of all the current interest, it must be asked: *What does the Bible teach concerning the Jubilee Year, and when will the next Jubilee Year occur?*

 THE BIBLICAL OBSERVANCE

The Sabbatical Year

To understand the Jubilee Year, one must first be familiar with the *Sabbatical Year*. The Sabbatical Year was known by several names in Scripture. Each highlighted an aspect of its observance. It was known as the *Seventh Year* since it was observed every seventh year (Ex. 23:11; Lev. 25:20; Dt. 15:9; Neh. 10:31; cf. 1 Macc. 6:53). It was also known as the *Sabbath of the Land* because the land was to have complete rest from cultivation for the year (Lev. 25:4, 6; 26:34, 43). Finally, the Sabbatical Year was known as the *Year of Release* because farming and debt payment were released (discontinued) for the year (Dt. 15:1-2; 31:10).

The Requirements of the Sabbatical Year

The Lord outlined several requirements for the Sabbatical Year. **First,** it was to be a sabbath year of rest *for the land* (Ex. 23:10-11) much like the sabbath day of rest *for man* (Ex. 23:12). The Sabbatical Year was the seventh year in a "week" of years. During the Sabbatical Year all cultivation activities were forbidden. There was to be no plowing, no sowing, and no tending to the grapevines or olive trees (Ex. 23:10-11; Lev. 25:2-5).

The Lord promised an extra bountiful harvest in the sixth year so that it could be stored as provision for the seventh year. This was similar to the double portion of manna which He gave to Israel in the wilderness on the sixth day so that there would be provision for the seventh day (Sabbath). The Sabbatical Year was a regular reminder for Israel to look to the Lord for even the most basic needs of life.

Sabbatical years began in the month of Tishri (September/October), coinciding with the civil New Year. The prohibition on working the land became effective thirty days before this since cultivation activities at the end of the sixth year would be preparation for the seventh year's crops. This prohibition against cultivating the land traditionally applied only to land within Israel (Lev. 25:2), not Jewish-held land in foreign countries.

Second, any crops that sprang up naturally by themselves in the seventh year were to be accessible to anyone in the community (Ex. 23:11; Lev. 25:6-7). Ownership could not be exercised over these volunteer crops.

Third, any produce which grew of itself during a Sabbatical Year could be eaten only in season. It could not be stored for future use since reaping (harvesting for the purpose of storage) was strictly forbidden (Lev. 25:5).

Fourth, debts were released in a Sabbatical Year (Dt. 15:1-4). The Sabbatical Year was a special grace period in which debt service was not pressed. The debts themselves were not erased, only the payments during a Sabbatical Year. Since the fields could not be worked, income could not be earned from farming and, therefore, debt payment was postponed. However, foreign debtors were not released from debt payment to Israelites during a Sabbatical Year (Dt. 15:3) since foreigners were able to farm their lands.

Fifth, in a Sabbatical Year, the Law of the Lord was to be read aloud to the people during the Feast of Tabernacles (Dt. 31:10-13, cf. Neh. 8:2, 13-18).

All families in the economic structure of ancient Israel were small business owners. In the extreme circumstance where a debt was incurred that could not be repaid, it was permissible for the debtor to hire himself into the employment of the creditor (bondslavery) as a last resort. Some have mistakenly assumed that all Israelite bondslaves were to be released during a Sabbatical Year to return to the care of their own businesses. However, this was not the case. The Scriptures state that Jewish bondslaves were to be released from bondage in the seventh service year of their particular employment (Ex. 21:2; Dt. 15:12). This is not to be confused with the seventh year for the land (Sabbatical Year). Ancient Jewish opinion was agreed upon this interpretation (Talmud Yerushalmi, Kiddushin 1:2, 59a).

The History of the Sabbatical Year

The Lord warned that if Israel refused to keep these laws, He would send them into captivity so that "Then the land shall enjoy its sabbaths as long as it lies desolate and you are in your enemies' land" (Lev. 26:34). In the early days of the nation, Israel did not heed the Lord's command to observe the Sabbatical Year. As a consequence, He carried them away into Babylon for seventy years, "until the land had enjoyed her Sabbaths" (2 Chr. 36:21).

History reveals that the Sabbatical Year was carefully observed after the return from Babylonian captivity. Israel solemnly swore to keep the Sabbatical Year in the days of Nehemiah (Neh. 10:31). Under Grecian rule, Israel was exempt from paying tribute to Alexander the Great during Sabbatical years (ca. 324 B.C.; *Antiquities of the Jews* 11.8.5-6). Two centuries later, the Sabbatical Year was still faithfully observed during Jewish independence (ca. 165-135 B.C.; 1 Macc. 6:49, 53; *Antiquities of the Jews* 13.8.1; *Wars of the Jews* 1.2.4). Later, the Romans continued the Grecian policy of waiving tribute taxes for Judea during Sabbatical years (*Antiquities of the Jews* 14.10.6). Finally, history records that Herod's siege of Jerusalem was especially severe because of a food shortage due to a Sabbatical Year (ca. 37 B.C.; *Antiquities of the Jews* 14.16.2).

After the destruction of the Temple in A.D. 70, the Sabbatical Year was not widely observed since most Jewish people were dispersed outside the land of Israel. This eventually led to an uncertainty as to the timing of the Sabbatical Year and many debates among the rabbis. As uncertain as the correct timing may be, the Sabbatical Year continues to be calculated today; however, very few within the modern State of Israel actually observe it. The last full Sabbatical Year of the twentieth century began September 16, 1993.

The Jubilee Year

Israel's other holy year was the Jubilee Year. Its timing was to years what the timing of Shavuot is to days. The Jubilee Year occurred every fiftieth year, the year after seven Sabbatical years or weeks of years had passed (Lev. 25:8-11). Shavuot occurs on the fiftieth day, the day after seven weeks pass from Firstfruits.

Some have suggested that the Jubilee Year was in reality a forty-ninth year, a special Sabbatical Year. Support is sought in the Book of Jubilees which counted a Jubilee as only 49 years. However, this clearly contradicts the inspired Word of God which specifies the Jubilee as a distinct fiftieth year (Lev. 25:10-11). Others have postulated that the Jubilee Year was the fiftieth year and also the first year in the counting of the next sabbatical cycle. This, too, finds no biblical support. In addition, the overwhelming majority of ancient Jewish sages clearly taught that the Jubilee Year was the fiftieth year (when seven sabbatical cycles were complete) and distinct from the first year in the next sabbatical cycle (Nedarim 61a; Talmud Yerushalmi, Kiddushin 1:2, 59a). Seven complete sabbatical cycles preceded each Jubilee Year, and seven complete cycles followed it.

The Jubilee Year is known as *Yovel* in Hebrew. Many believe that the origin of the word is from the Hebrew word for "ram" (cf. Josh. 6:5) since the blowing of the ram's horn on Yom Kippur proclaimed the beginning of the Jubilee Year (Lev. 25:9). Josephus believed that the word denoted "liberty" (*Antiquities of the Jews* 3.12.3).

The Requirements of the Jubilee Year

The primary laws for the Sabbatical Year also held true for the Jubilee Year. The land was to remain at rest, ownership could not be claimed for any produce in the fields, and produce in a Jubilee Year could not be stored for future use (Lev. 25:11-12). The Lord graciously promised a triple crop in the sixth year of the last sabbatical cycle to provide for the back-to-back fallow years (a Sabbatical and Jubilee Year) until the "ninth year," the year after the Jubilee (Lev. 25:20-22).

Scripture gave three additional requirements for the Jubilee Year. **First**, the shofar (ram's horn) was to be blown on Yom Kippur to announce that the Jubilee Year had commenced (Lev. 25:9).

Second, all hired workers were to be set free (Lev. 25:39-54). This was unconditional liberty. All bondslaves were released even if the Jubilee Year came before the completion of their six years of service. This also included bondslaves who had earlier declined to go free in the seventh year of their employment. All were set at liberty.

Third, all land was to be returned to its original owner (Lev. 25:13, 23-28). This law preserved the identity of the tribes and their allotted inheritance of the land (Num. 36:4, 7).

The primary reason for the Jubilee Year was to prevent oppression in Israel (Lev. 25:14, 17). An Israelite could hire himself into the service of another to retire a debt, but he had no right to sell himself or his family forever into slavery. The Lord alone owned the sons of Israel since He had redeemed them out of Egypt (Lev. 25:42, 55). In similar fashion, an Israelite could lease his land for a term of years, but he had no right to permanently sell his tribal inheritance. The Lord alone owned the land of Israel (Lev. 25:23), and He had allotted it among the tribes. These were indisputable facts. God, as Sovereign King of the universe, owned the people and the land.

The Jubilee Year restored the economic structure of Israel's society as it had been when God brought them into the land. Tribal identity was maintained, land remained in the hands of small landholders, and people were set free to develop their own businesses.

The History of the Jubilee Year

The observance of the Jubilee Year, like that of the Sabbatical Year, was also neglected during Israel's early history. In fact, *there is no historical record, biblical or extrabiblical, that Israel ever once observed the Jubilee Year*. Josephus often cited Sabbatical Year observance, but never that of the Jubilee Year.

The ancient rabbis generally believed that the Jubilee was no longer in effect after the exile of the northern ten tribes (722 B.C.) since the biblical command for observance was for "all the inhabitants thereof" (Lev. 25:10).

They believed that the Jubilee Year applied only when all the Jewish people were in the land, with each tribe in its own territory. Perhaps this is the reason that only the Sabbatical Year (not the Jubilee Year) was mentioned in the people's solemn oath in the time of Nehemiah (Neh. 10:31).

Permit it to be stated once again: There are no firm historical records upon which to base the date for a Jubilee Year. Even if there were, the resulting calculations would be highly uncertain due to the national catastrophes of the Assyrian exile, the Babylonian captivity, and the Roman destruction of the Temple and resulting dispersion. Did the reckoning of the Jubilee continue when Israel was out of the land? If not, did the cycle resume where it left off, or begin anew when Israel returned? Since the timing is not known today, the shofar (ram's horn) is blown in the synagogue as a memorial of the Jubilee Year at the close of Yom Kippur each year.

Therefore, to try to predict the year of Messiah's coming based upon the timing of the Jubilee Year is an exercise in futility. It is impossible to know the timing of the Jubilee Year today since any calculation must *assume* a starting year.

But a more basic problem exists for the date-setters: The Bible does not state that the Messiah must return in a Jubilee Year. That is simply an unsubstantiated assumption.

THE FUTURE FULFILLMENT

The fulfillment of the Jubilee Year is to be found, not in its timing, but in the prophetic truth which it portrays. The Jubilee Year looks to the restoration of Israel by the Messiah and to the resulting messianic Kingdom of peace. But how will this be accomplished?

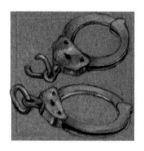

The Oppression of Israel Will Be Ended

Israel has been under the yoke of Gentile domination at least since the beginning of the Babylonian captivity in 586 B.C. (although a case could also be made for the Assyrian exile of 722 B.C.). Even today, two out of every three Jewish people live under Gentile rule. Because of the nations, Israel possesses only a very small portion of the Promised Land, has no Temple, and cannot even pray on the Temple Mount, to which King David holds the title deed.

Daniel prophesied that Gentile oppression would become unbelievably severe at the end of this age. A wicked Gentile ruler will arise and "he shall exalt and magnify himself above every god, shall speak blasphemies against the God of gods" (Dan. 11:36). This ruler will bring terrible persecution upon Israel: "A time of trouble, Such as never was since there was a nation, Even to that time. And at that time your people shall be delivered" (Dan. 12:1).

The prophet Jeremiah also spoke of this "time of Jacob's trouble" and likewise promised that Israel would be delivered (Jer. 30:4-7). He foretold: "'For it shall come to pass in that day,' Says the LORD of hosts, 'That I will break his [the wicked ruler's] yoke from your [Israel's] neck, And will burst your bonds; Foreigners shall no more enslave them. But they [Israel] shall serve the LORD their God, And David their king [Messiah], Whom I will raise up for them'" (Jer. 30:8-9).

The Lord similarly promised through yet another Jewish prophet: "It shall come to pass in that day That his [the wicked ruler's] burden will be taken away from your shoulder, And his yoke from your neck, And the yoke will be destroyed because of the anointing oil" (Isa. 10:27). The ancient Jewish viewpoint (Targum Jonathan) interpreted "the anointing oil" (lit. "oily one") to be a reference to the Messiah (Anointed One) and His deliverance of Israel from the yoke of Gentile oppression.

When Messiah comes, He will break the chains of Israel's oppression. But this deliverance will come only when the nation has first repented of her sin. The nation must repent (Yom Kippur) before the shofar will sound the release of her captivity (the Jubilee Year). This sequence is necessary since sin is the root of the oppression as the Lord declared: "Which of My creditors is it to whom I have sold you? For your iniquities you have sold yourselves" (Isa. 50:1). In Messiah's glorious day, Israel will return to the Lord and, subsequently, will no longer be the bondslaves of the nations, but the redeemed servants of the Living God. Israel's oppression will be ended.

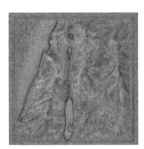

The Ownership of Israel Will Be Restored

When Messiah comes, the great shofar will be blown, and the exiles of Israel will be regathered to their land. There will be no controversy over access to the Temple Mount, as the Hebrew prophet spoke: "So it shall be in that day: The great trumpet [shofar] will be blown; They will come, who are about to perish in the land of Assyria, And they who are outcasts in the land of Egypt, And shall worship the LORD *in the holy mount at Jerusalem*" (Isa. 27:13). Neither will there be controversy over the ownership of the land, as the Lord promised: "The Lord GOD will blow the trumpet [shofar] . . . . The LORD their God will save them in that day, As the flock of His people. For they shall be like the jewels of a crown, Lifted like a banner over *His land*" (Zech. 9:14-16).

The prophet foretold that when Messiah comes to "raise up the tribes of Jacob, And to restore the preserved ones of Israel" (Isa. 49:6), He will also "cause them to inherit the desolate heritages" (Isa. 49:8; cf. Ezek. 47:13-48:29; Amos 9:14-15; Obad. 17). In other words, Messiah will apportion the land of Israel (the desolate tribal inheritances) and restore it to the tribes of Jacob. In the end, it is the Lord alone who owns the land, and He has chosen to give it to Abraham and his descendants "as an everlasting possession" (Gen. 17:8).

Men will continue to work feverishly at their Middle East peace plans, but in the end, they will not succeed, because the Lord has His peace plan. It is embodied in the Son of David. All history is moving toward the return of Messiah.

In that day, Satan will be banished (Ezek. 28:2, 8, 13-19), and the rebellion of wicked men will be crushed (Ps. 2:9). In that day, the sons of Israel "shall trust in the name of the LORD" (Zeph. 3:12) and "walk in the name of the LORD our God Forever and ever" (Mic. 4:5). And in that day, Messiah shall establish the throne of David and the messianic Kingdom "even forever" (Isa. 9:7).

Finally, in Messiah's glorious day, there will be Jubilee rest for the land and freedom for God's people. Everyone shall sit "under his vine and under his fig tree . . . [of this be very sure] For the mouth of the LORD of hosts has spoken" (Mic. 4:4).

Jewish Holiday Schedule

Year	Passover	Shavuot	Rosh Hashanah	Yom Kippur	Sukkot	Tisha B'Av	Hanukkah	Purim
1995	Apr 15	Jun 4	Sep 25	Oct 4	Oct 9	Aug 6	Dec 18	Mar 16
1996	Apr 4	May 24	Sep 14	Sep 23	Sep 28	Jul 25	Dec 6	Mar 5
1997	Apr 22	Jun 11	Oct 2	Oct 11	Oct 16	Aug 12	Dec 24	Mar 23
1998	Apr 11	May 31	Sep 21	Sep 30	Oct 5	Aug 2	Dec 14	Mar 12
1999	Apr 1	May 21	Sep 11	Sep 20	Sep 25	Jul 22	Dec 4	Mar 2
2000	Apr 20	Jun 9	Sep 30	Oct 9	Oct 14	Aug 10	Dec 22	Mar 21
2001	Apr 8	May 28	Sep 18	Sep 27	Oct 2	Jul 29	Dec 10	Mar 9
2002	Mar 28	May 17	Sep 7	Sep 16	Sep 21	Jul 18	Nov 30	Feb 26
2003	Apr 17	Jun 6	Sep 27	Oct 6	Oct 11	Aug 7	Dec 20	Mar 18
2004	Apr 6	May 26	Sep 16	Sep 25	Sep 30	Jul 27	Dec 8	Mar 7
2005	Apr 24	Jun 13	Oct 4	Oct 13	Oct 18	Aug 14	Dec 26	Mar 25
2006	Apr 13	Jun 2	Sep 23	Oct 2	Oct 7	Aug 3	Dec 16	Mar 14
2007	Apr 3	May 23	Sep 13	Sep 22	Sep 27	Jul 24	Dec 5	Mar 4
2008	Apr 20	Jun 9	Sep 30	Oct 9	Oct 14	Aug 10	Dec 22	Mar 21
2009	Apr 9	May 29	Sep 19	Sep 28	Oct 3	Jul 30	Dec 12	Mar 10
2010	Mar 30	May 19	Sep 9	Sep 18	Sep 23	Jul 20	Dec 2	Feb 28
2011	Apr 19	Jun 8	Sep 29	Oct 8	Oct 13	Aug 9	Dec 21	Mar 20
2012	Apr 7	May 27	Sep 17	Sep 26	Oct 1	Jul 29	Dec 9	Mar 8
2013	Mar 26	May 15	Sep 5	Sep 14	Sep 19	Jul 16	Nov 28	Feb 24
2014	Apr 15	Jun 4	Sep 25	Oct 4	Oct 9	Aug 5	Dec 17	Mar 16
2015	Apr 4	May 24	Sep 14	Sep 23	Sep 28	Jul 26	Dec 7	Mar 5
2016	Apr 23	Jun 12	Oct 3	Oct 12	Oct 17	Aug 14	Dec 25	Mar 24
2017	Apr 11	May 31	Sep 21	Sep 30	Oct 5	Aug 1	Dec 13	Mar 12
2018	Mar 31	May 20	Sep 10	Sep 19	Sep 24	Jul 22	Dec 3	Mar 1
2019	Apr 20	Jun 9	Sep 30	Oct 9	Oct 14	Aug 11	Dec 23	Mar 21
2020	Apr 9	May 29	Sep 19	Sep 28	Oct 3	Jul 30	Dec 11	Mar 10

BIBLIOGRAPHY

Agnon, S. Y. *Days of Awe*. New York: Schocken Books, 1965.

Danziger, Yehezkel (ed.). *The Mishnah, Seder Zeraim* Vol. III(b). Brooklyn: Mesorah Publications, Ltd., 1993.

De Sola Pool, David. *The Traditional Prayer Book for Sabbath and Festivals*. New Hyde Park: University Books, 1960.

Edersheim, Alfred. *The Temple*. Grand Rapids: Wm. B. Eerdmans Publishing Company, 1972.

Glaser, Mitch, and Zhava Glaser. *The Fall Feasts of Israel*. Chicago: Moody Press, 1987.

Goldwurm, Hersh, Meir Zlotowitz, and Nosson Scherman. *Chanukah*. Brooklyn: Mesorah Publications, Ltd., 1981.

Goldwurm, Hersh, Avie Gold, and Nosson Scherman. *Rosh Hashanah*. Brooklyn: Mesorah Publications, Ltd., 1983.

Goodman, Philip. *The Purim Anthology*. Philadelphia: The Jewish Publication Society, 1949.

——. *The Rosh Hashanah Anthology*. Philadelphia: The Jewish Publication Society, 1970.

——. *The Shavuot Anthology*. Philadelphia: The Jewish Publication Society, 1974.

Grunfeld, Dayan I. *Shemittah and Yobel*. New York: The Soncino Press, 1972.

Josephus, Flavius. *The Complete Works of Josephus*. Translated by William Whiston, Grand Rapids: Kregel Publications, 1960.

Kolatch, Alfred J. *The Jewish Book of Why*. New York: Jonathan David Publishers, 1981.

Rosen, Moishe, and Ceil Rosen. *Christ In The Passover*. Chicago: Moody Press, 1978.

Schauss, Hayyim. *The Jewish Festivals*. Translated by Samuel Jaffe, New York: Schocken Books, 1962.

Strassfeld, Michael. *The Jewish Holidays*. New York: Harper & Row, 1985.

GENERAL INDEX

lamb, Passover, 17, 18, 23, 44, 49-50, 51, 53, 57, 58, 61, 62, 69, 70, 78, 84, 85
lambs, 77, 81, 91, 104, 120, 131, 132, 136
Lamentations, 186
lampstand, see *menorah (lampstand)*
languages, 98-99
Last Supper, 58
   (see also *Upper Room; Passover*)
last things, 75
last trump, see under *Rosh Hashanah (Feast of Trumpets)*
laver, xi, 121-122
Law of Moses, see *Mosaic Law*
Law, tablets of, 97
leaven, 19, 22-23, 51, 54, 66-67, 68, 70, 71, 72, 78, 91
Leaven, Search for, ceremony, see *Bedikat Hametz*
Levites, 53, 57, 79, 84, 121, 139, 143, 172
Levitical choirs, 81, 108, 139, 140
Levitical feasts, see *feasts of the Lord*
libation ceremony, see under *Sukkot (Feast of Tabernacles)*
liberty, 196, 197
Life, Book of, see *Book of Life*
light, ascribed to Messiah, 141
living water, see *water, living*
Lord's Table, 27, 49, 59
   (see also *Last Supper*)
lots
   cast by Haman, 177, 181, 185
   used in Temple, 123
   (see also *Purim ([Feast of Lots])*)
Lots, Feast of, see *Purim (Feast of Lots)*
lunar calendar, Jewish, see *calendar*
luvav, see *branches used* under *Sukkot (Feast of Tabernacles)*
Lysimachus, 161

Maccabean dynasty, 166
Maccabean revolt, 164-166, 167
Maccabees, the, 138-139, 165-166, 170
   (see also under *Hanukkah [Feast of Dedication]*)
Maccabees, the Books of, 160
Macedonia, 160, 161
Malachi, 159
Malkhiyot, 111
manna, 194
Maoz Tzur, 169
Marduk (pagan deity), 179
maror, see *bitter herbs*
martyrs, 163-164, 172, 174
Mary, 84
Masada, 147
masquerades, 188
Matityahu, see *Mattathias*

Mattathias, 138, 164-165, 172
   see also *Maccabees; Hanukkah (Feast of Dedication)*
Matthew, 59, 172
matzah, see *unleavened bread (matzah)*
   (see also under *Passover*)
matzah tash, 53, 60
   (see also *unleavened bread*)
meal offerings, see under *offerings*
Medo-Persian Empire, 160, 171
Medo-Persian government, 179, 184
megillah, 186
   (see also *scrolls*)
Memorial of Blowing (of Trumpets), see *Zikhron Teruah*
Menelaus, 162
menorah (lampstand), 93, 121, 124, 140, 166, 167
Meron, 82-83
Messiah
   ascension of, 100, 129
   betrayal of, 58
   birth of, 172, 190
   burial of, 60, 69-70
   crucifixion of, 19, 99, 128
   death of, 23, 27, 49, 60, 62, 99, 100, 128, 131
   deity of, 172
   Elijah to announce coming of, 53, 59
   eternal reign on David's throne, 190, 200
   expectation, 142, 171-172
   false Messiahs
      Bar Kochba, 93, 105, 154
   first coming of, 15, 23, 25, 31, 86, 112, 175
   future restoration of Israel by, 129, 145, 157, 198-200
   future temple to be built by, 157
   Gentile oppression of Israel to be ended by, 129, 172, 190, 199
   Jesus' first public declaration as, 84
   Jew and Gentile one in, 22
   Jewish believers in, 61
   leader of Seder service in Upper Room, 55
   New Covenant instituted by, 23
   promise of, 175
   prophesied by King David and by Israel's prophets, 100
   rejected by Israel, 153, 171-172
   rejection prophesied, 60
   resurrection of, 20-22, 60, 69, 70, 86, 100
   sacrifice for sin, 69, 70, 85, 119, 127-128, 131-132, 133, 190
   second coming of, 15, 23, 26, 27, 28, 29, 31, 96, 111, 112, 114, 115, 116, 128, 129, 198, 200
   son of David, 200
   (see also *Jesus Christ*)
messianic Kingdom, 14, 23, 30, 31, 37-38, 44, 46,

SCRIPTURE INDEX

222

FOR FURTHER INFORMATION

Many individuals, after reading this book, may wish to receive further information on available materials concerning Bible prophecy and related topics. Kevin Howard is presently the field director of *ZION'S HOPE, Inc.*, a faith mission to the Jewish people. *ZION'S HOPE* publishes a bimonthly, Bible-teaching magazine, *Zion's Fire*, which deals with Israel and the prophetic Word. For information on other available materials or for a free one-year subscription to *Zion's Fire*, write: *ZION'S HOPE, Inc.*, P. O. Box 690909, Orlando, FL 32869; or call 1-800-4-ISRAEL (1-800-447-7235).